VERSES
OF
CADENCE

VERSES OF CADENCE

An Introduction to the Prosody of
Chaucer and his followers

by

JAMES G. SOUTHWORTH
Professor of English, University of Toledo

OXFORD
BASIL BLACKWELL
MCMLIV

PRINTED IN GREAT BRITAIN IN THE CITY OF OXFORD
AT THE VINCENT-BAXTER PRESS

This book is
affectionately dedicated
to
Jim and Hester, Jules and Phyllis
George and Teta, and Sophia

CONTENTS

CONTENTS

PREFACE

THE present study of the prosody of Chaucer and his followers is an attempt to return to fundamentals—to free Chaucer and the poets of the fifteenth century from the effects of certain fallacies of nineteenth-century scholars, fallacies, which have attained the status of myths. In the present case it is to place him in the poetic tradition to which he belongs and to remove him from a tradition that only began to come into existence in the sixteenth century. This confusion of traditions has sired several other fallacies or myths which have achieved the stature of proved facts, although they have never been proved. Scholars are dedicated to detect fallacies. In their treatment of Chaucer's prosody, the nineteenth-century scholars created them.

A nation's poetic tradition is not always so simple as many scholars believe. Because of the English tendency to borrow freely, the English tradition is complicated in detail but simple in outline. The tradition is continuous from our earliest poetry, but it is one that has been constantly modified by foreign influences which, however, have never wholly destroyed the original —nor even obscured it to the poets. Modern poets, for example, like T. S. Eliot, Wallace Stevens, William Carlos Williams, Ezra Pound, Stephen Spender—to name but a few—have, perhaps unconscious of their historic role, done much to restore English poetry to its native tradition. I think it can be said with a great measure of truth that the native tradition is found unchecked in *Piers Plowman*, checked and altered in the poetry of Chaucer. In both it is a rhythmical rather than a metrical tradition. With Surrey the tradition is altered, but not basically changed. Although contemporary writers begin to use classical terms and to speak of feet, poets continue to write in units longer than the foot. Music exerts a stronger influence than classical prosody.

Throughout the sixteenth, seventeenth, eighteenth, and most of the nineteenth centuries, poets recognized the rhythmical tradition of Chaucer, although they themselves became increasingly under the dominance of the metrical. At the end of the eighteenth century, however, scholars began to suspect the tradition accepted by the poets and began to try to make

1

Chaucer a "correct" poet, a correct poet being one whose decasyllables were, theoretically at least, in iambic pentameter.
Urry was the first to attempt to apply to Chaucer metrical
criteria which had their origins with the sixteenth-century
humanistic study of classical meters; but his efforts bore little
immediate fruit. Tyrwhitt suggested a different metrical basis
—the endecasyllabic, but the untenability of his suggestions
was exposed by Nott in 1815. It is clear from the *Biographia
Literaria* that Coleridge agreed with Nott. Not until the studies
of Child, Ellis, Schipper, Ten Brink, and others, however, was
the rhythmical nature of Chaucer's prosody again challenged.
It will be apparent from the present study that because of a lack
of historical perspective, and because of the use of unsupported
assumptions and faulty logic, these scholars succeeded in imposing on Chaucer and his followers the myth of a metrical
prosody. This was essentially a "scholarly" movement. The
imposition of the myth of a metrical prosody was not accom-
plished, however, without the greatest difficulty, and only by
ignoring the evidence provided by the MSS of Chaucer, Hoccleve,
and others, and by thinking of Chaucer as working outside the
English tradition. It will surprise many persons to discover
how much of the accepted data of Middle English phonology,
particularly that of Chaucer, rests on shaky foundations. As the
late Professor Bloomfield is reported as having said in private—
Middle English phonology was a mess. Professor Manly also
realized that a re-examination was in order.

The present study makes no attempt at definitiveness, neither
definitiveness in the analysis of the linguistic studies nor of the
prosody of Chaucer's followers. I have merely indicated the
route further investigators may wish to pursue. I hope, however, that I have offered sufficient illustrative material to support
my statements, and that I have asked some of the important
questions. Wherever one turns, the abundance of evidence for
answering those questions as I have suggested they should be
answered is surprisingly great. There are other questions, too,
for which I have not attempted to find an answer. Have not
the linguists, for example, by their adherence to a wrong prosodic basis for Chaucer tended to obscure the real relationships
between the dialects of the North, the Midlands, and the South,
particularly in the matter of the time of the disappearance of

final -*e* ? The answers can only be found, however, in the MSS or printed texts not edited on a preconceived prosodic principle. The texts of the Chaucer Society were not so edited. By a return to original sources the student will have brought more forcefully to his attention the truth of the matter of the following pages. In almost every case I have had recourse to microfilms or photostats when the originals were not available.

My indebtednesses are many, both to those who have given encouragement and to those who have remained obstinate. From the latter I have perhaps learned more. Their inertia and apathy and their satisfaction with theories they learned in their college days have forced me to go more deeply into the question than was needed for my own conviction.

I am constantly impressed with the unfailing courtesy of the staffs of our libraries. My thanks are due to those of Harvard College, the Huntington Library, University of Michigan, University of Chicago (particularly Miss Mabel Dean), and the University of Toledo (particularly Miss Lucille Emch). I can only continue to thank Professor Hyder Rollins for his counsel, advice, and encouragement over many years. I know of no director of graduate students who does more for the men privileged to work under him than he. To him and to the late Dr. A. J. Carlyle, my Oxford tutor, I shall always remain greatly indebted. To Dr. Ernest Gray my indebtedness is of a different order. He has made many valuable textual suggestions, most of which I have adopted. Elizabeth Gould, concert pianist and composer, has verified my musical notations.

CHAPTER ONE

A PROBLEM IN PROSODY

IT is difficult to write on any prosodic subject even when no
question exists about the pronunciation of the language; it is
more difficult to write on the subject when, as Professor Baum
has said in " The Metre of Beowulf," the field "is already occupied
by a theory which, in spite of various modifications, has for
many years taken on an aspect of authority". And, he adds,
"if there is any discipline in which it behooves us to move
cautiously and to beware of the assumption of certainty, it is
the prosody of a dead language" (*ML*, XLVI, 73, 74). In spite
of changes in pronunciation, the language of Chaucer is still a
vital, living language, but to earlier investigators it had practically achieved the status of a dead one. Had these earlier
investigators—Child, Schipper, Ten Brink, and Skeat, to name
but a few—not begun with what Professor Fredson Bowers calls
the "Teutonic method of establishing out of thin air a hypothetical *typus*, and then surveying the differences between the
thing which is not and the actual facts", the whole attitude
towards the prosody of Chaucer and the fifteenth century would
probably be different. The scholar whose ear has become at-
tuned to the music of modern rhythms as manifested in the work
of Eliot, Pound, Williams, Stevens, Ransom, Marianne Moore,
Auden, Spender, and Thomas will be far more reluctant to
establish a *typus* than were the late nineteenth-century investigators, because he is acutely aware of the fact that the rhythms
of poetry are based on the rhythms of prose. The problems our
modern poets have faced are the same problems that Chaucer
had to face—that every original poet has to face. He had to find
an instrument to suit his subject matter. There was but a single
choice open to him—to modify one of the already existing forms
of the prosodic line so as to capture the rhythms of contemporary
prose. As Professor Baum has said of the *Beowulf* poet—he
"composed as other poets have been known to compose and that
metre was for him, as for later poets, a highly organized prose;
for in English certainly the tunes and modulations of prose are
the basis of all metrical language . . ." (*Ibid.*, 74). Or, as the late
Professor Raleigh said, "No poet makes his own language. No
poet introduces serious or numerous modifications into the langu-

age that he uses. Some, no doubt, coin words and revive them, like Spenser or Keats in verse, Carlyle or Sir Thomas Browne in prose. But least of all great poets did Chaucer mould and modify the speech he found. The poets who take liberties with speech are either prophets or eccentrics. From either of these characters Chaucer was far removed. He held fast by communal and social standards for literary speech. His English is plain, terse, homely, colloquial English, taken alive *out of daily speech*" (Quoted in John Speirs, *Chaucer the Maker*, 1951, p. 18). Raleigh was right, and should examples be necessary, Miss Schlauch provides them in her "Chaucer's Colloquial English: Its Structural Traits" (*PMLA*, LXVII, December 1952, 1103—1116). Or, to quote Mr. Speirs, ". . . Chaucer's genius, like Shakespeare's, is rooted in the English language as it was spoken in his time. Chaucer's English is unmistakably the English of cultivated people; it is unmistakably rooted in the speech of an agricultural folk. . . . Yet the completely English Chaucer was closely associated with his contemporary Court" (p. 19).

I think most scholars agree that in the London speech of Chaucer's day final unaccented -e had died out, and that Chaucer's use of it was a conscious archaism. Mr. Donaldson ("Chaucer's Final -E", *PMLA*, LXIII (December, 1948), 1101—1124) adopted a more conservative view about the state of final -e in English than did I ("Chaucer's Final -E in Rhyme", *PMLA*, LXII (December, 1947), 910—935). The actual difference in Mr. Donaldson's and my point of view was the extent of this archaism. I now think that we were both wrong, the reason lying in the fact that we had both accepted the iambic decasyllabic verse as the basis for Chaucer's prosody. He would allow fewer substitutions of anapests and trochees than would I. I now find highly unrealistic the concept current among traditional linguists that Chaucer purposely used a more archaic English in his verse than in his prose. Poets simply do not work in this way, nor did the earlier investigators think so. This is one of the minor effects of the Teutonic method of establishing a *typus*. If, then, Chaucer did not pronounce his final unaccented *e*'s, the iambic-decasyllabic hypothesis is no longer feasible. What, then, was Chaucer's prosodic basis ?

The tenableness of the iambic-decasyllabic hypothesis is the basic problem confronting us. But since the metrical theories—either endecasyllabic or that of iambic pentameter—have exerted a profound effect on the phonology of Middle English grammar, and still do in that of Chaucer, a brief review of some of the pertinent facts is necessary. The main difference between my approach to Chaucer's prosody and that of other scholars is, like Professor Baum's to *Beowulf*, "One of attitude; a disbelief in laws and rules as the nineteenth-century understood such things and a conviction that prosody is to be approached in a less rigorous and dogmatic spirit. The chief merit is . . . thus its freedom from over-formalism and its allowance for just the same kind of variety and 'irregularity' as that which we recognize in our study of metre in the modern Germanic languages" (162).

It will be obvious that any study of Chaucer and his followers cannot be based on any text edited according to any preconceived prosodic principle. It must be based on the facts as exhibited in the MSS. Unfortunately the published materials are scant. Manly and Rickert's edition of the *Canterbury Tales*, Henry Bergen's edition of Lydgate's *Fall of Princes*, W. M. Mackenzie's edition of *The Kingis Quair*, and Miss Foxwell's edition of the poems of Wyatt are satisfactory. Although Miss Foxwell did not edit the text on any preconceived metrical basis, she is often incorrect in details; fortunately, I have had access to the edition of Richard Harrier, still in MS. It is to be regretted, however, and I know other scholars share my opinion, that both Manly and Bergen decided against the use of the virgule (/) which occurs in the best MSS. As I shall have occasion to point out, the purpose of the virgule was not, as nineteenth-century scholars would have it, to indicate the caesura; it is a definite aid in determining the rhetorical pattern of the line and invaluable to the person reading aloud. Both Nott and Payne realized that its purpose was to indicate the "sectional pause". When I speak of nineteenth-century scholars I am speaking generally, of course, because what few persons realize is that Child and his supporters were fought at every turn by the conservative group who believed that Child and his supporters were imposing a metrical pattern on Chaucer that was contrary to the facts. In other words, the theory which I shall advance is that substantially held by Nott and Price, and rediscovered about Lydgate by Mr. C. S. Lewis ("The Fifteenth Century Heroic Line", *ESEA*, XXIV, 28—41), and which was the basis of Spenser's attempted imitation of Chaucer in the February eclogue. The linguistic studies of Payne, Weymouth, and others lend the support of historical grammar to the theory.

Any study of Chaucer's prosody that can lay claim to validity must do certain things. First, it must show that the characteristics of Chaucer's language were the same as those of the London English of his day because it is inconceivable that Chaucer would be eccentric in his pronunciation. Second, it must examine the possible models available to the poet. Third, it must examine the evidence of the MS texts. And, fourth, it must examine the MS texts of his avowed disciples. At times, the investigator must ignore certain conventions accepted by grammarians if he can show that those rules were based on assumptions that have never been proved true. Particularly, this will apply to the pronunciation or non-pronunciation of final unaccented -e, which is in a "deep slumber of decided opinion". If such a study of the four conditions reveals a prosodic system that satisfies *all without the necessity of any emendation*, then that system deserves precedence over one that fails to satisfy them.

Prosodists are in general agreement that the application of quantitative terms to English verse is inaccurate. The tendency to use such terms as iamb, trochee, and so forth, had its origin, says T. S. Omond (*English Metrists*, Oxford, 1921), in the enthusiasm of the young Cambridge scholars who had lately discovered Greek literature—Ascham, Cheke, Watson, and others. Cheke and Ascham, he says, probably "taught orally to their pupils the expediency of adopting quantitative measures". This, he adds, later led to the Areopagus in the late sixteenth century with Sidney, Dyer, and Drant as leaders, and was essentially a scholar's movement. Whether the Areopagus actually existed is still a debatable question. It is not strange considering their strong bias that these metrists, trying to advance the cause of classical measures, would have little understanding of Chaucer's rhythms. We must be careful, however, not to underestimate the knowledge of men like Ascham, Puttenham, King James, and others in prosodic matters. The term *foot*, for example, was an ambiguous term to them (See Ing, *Elizabethan Lyrics*, 35—40; 68), and we must be certain that we understand how each used it. We must recognize, however, that Elizabethan prosodists paid at least lip service to the natural accent of normal pronunciation of English, and by doing so must have made some use of ordinary speech in the construction of their verse.

Miss Ing has demonstrated in the chapter "Elizabethan Lyrics and Music" (*Ibid.*, 107—150) that to enjoy many lyrics of that age, "it is essential to allow whole phrases to remain undivided by any attempt at ordering into simple repeating 'feet', and to read the phrases with sufficient care to make their rhythm perceptible" (121). What is true of many of these lyrics is likewise true, I think, of much of Shakespeare's dramatic as well as lyric verse. Another unfortunate misconception arose from the failure of the Romans to understand the nature of Greek iambic verse. "The Iambic line," says M. A. Bayfield (*The Measures of the Poets*, Cambridge, 1919), "corresponds to our heroic line in being the staple measure of Greek Tragedy and Comedy. From a failure to distinguish between Metre and Rhythm, it was in Roman times, when Greek prosody was little understood, supposed to be composed of iambi. . . . To this fundamental error, which was shared and handed down by Horace (*Ars Poetica*, 251 ff.), and blindly accepted by the literary world at the Revival of Learning, the present hopeless condition of English prosody is largely if not entirely due" (7).

The great objection to the use of the classical terminology is that it fails to take into consideration the time aspect of English verse. And it is just that time aspect that is so important a part of the beauty of English poetry, as it is of its prose. Without it we cannot have a proper understanding of the *rhythm* of English verse, a matter much neglected by those who make too facile a use of classical terms. By *rhythm*, of course, is not meant counting syllables and measuring the distance between accents. We have rhythm when a passage, read aloud, to quote Fowler, " falls naturally into groups of words each well fitted by its length and intonation for its place in the whole and its relation to its neighbours." I am not here speaking of quantitative verse as understood in classical prosody. I shall employ in the present discussion both the system devised by William Thompson (*Rhythms of Speech*, 1924) which gives a more accurate picture of the facts than the classical terminology gives and the traditional notation. English poetry is essentially in 3/8 rhythm, or multiples thereof, although occasionally a combination of 3/8 and 2/8 does occur. Different readers will read many of the lines

differently from the way I do.   I do not always read the same
lines in the same way.   But the difference will be and is a rhetori-
cal difference.   The vertical bar (|) before the vowel indicates a
strong stress; a broken bar (⁞) a lighter one.   The traditional
iamb is represented thus: ♪| ♩.   Actually, in English verse, the
unaccented syllable may be twice as long as the stressed syllable:
and often is ♩|♪.   Strictly speaking, this is not an iamb.   For
the sake of simplicity I have made little attempt to indicate the
degree of stress and generally employ the solid bar.   I cannot
overstress the fact, however, that since the emphasis in reading
is largely a subjective matter, no two readers will agree in all
details of their musical notation.   Occasionally I even employ
a rest—ㄱ.   Merely because we often have lines with a fairly
regular alternation of unstressed and stressed syllables we must
not mistake this for the division of the line into feet.   Modern
studies of Chaucer's prosody have suffered, I believe, from the
persistence of certain misconceptions.   In *An English Prosody
on Inductive Lines* (Cambridge, 1928), Sir George Young indulges
in several unsupported generalizations.   In Chapter Two he
claims, for example, that the distinctive quality of Chaucer's
contribution is the "utter negation of any normal break or
division of the line into hemistichs.   It is to this negation that
the line has owed its beauty, and its capability for later development" (11).   One of the results of the present investigation will
be to show that what Sir George claims for the line did not occur
until Surrey.   Had he said that Chaucer tended to *minimize* the
division of the line into hemistichs, I should not disagree with him.

He stresses, moreover, that "it is the line, and not the ar-
rangement of the lines, whether in stanza, or by couplet, which
constitutes his great achievement".   This statement would indicate that he accepts the single-verse as the unit of measurement.   Mr. E. Talbot Donaldson in his attempted refutation of
my "Chaucer's Final -E in Rhyme" also insisted that the single-
verse unit be accepted.   Since the two statements of Sir George
derive from and perpetuate myths, let us begin our study of
Chaucer's prosody by examining the origin of these myths, their
cause, and their makers.   These myths retain abundant vitality
in every Middle English Grammar, sections of which badly need
revision.   Let us begin with the myth of the single-verse as a unit
of measurement.

CHAPTER TWO

MYTHS AND MYTH-MAKERS

i. *The Myth of the Single-Verse Unit*

CLASSICAL authority is definitely opposed to the single-verse unit theory. Plato would oppose it because he insists that the sound and rhythm of poetry must be subordinate to language—the logos (*Republic*, 398 *e d*; also 400 *a d*). Aristotle specifically mentions in his *Rhetoric* (III, ix), a work almost certainly known by Chaucer, that the period and not the verse must be the unit of measurement. Longinus in *On the Sublime* (XXXIX, XL), which Chaucer probably did not know, insists on the unity and harmony of the whole passage. The harmony could only be achieved by the building of phrase upon phrase and the collocation of all members.

In French the single verse could not be the unit of measurement because, according to Arthur Gosset, "French verse has only two dimensions, rhyme and metre; so that, if one takes away the rhyme, it becomes invisible—in other words, indistinguishable from prose" (*A Manual of French Prosody*, 1884). And as Leon Gautier points out (*Les Épopées Françaises*, 3 vols., Paris, 1865-68), in French a verse comprised what we call a couplet: "Les poëtes du moyen âge appelaient *vers* ce que nous appelons couplet" (I, 310). Moreover, he adds, "chaque couplet forme parfois à lui seul une espèce de petit poëme" (I, 219). In the French *Chasteau d'Amour*, the only punctuation, says Weymouth (*Philol. Soc. Trans.*, 1865, p. 4), was a comma at the end of each couplet. A more conclusive illustration of the fact that a single verse was not considered a unit even when not a couplet appears in Machaut's *Le Livre*. We have his own musical notation for the following:

> Dame se vous n'avez apercéu
> Que je vous aim de cuer, sans decevoir,
> Essaiez-le, si la sarez de voir

p. 152

The musical phrase is continuous until after "decevoir": ". . . voir" is held for a dotted whole note, and is followed by the rest of a whole bar. I mention this aspect of French prosody now

because of its possible influence on Chaucer.   Later, we shall
consider the possibility of the influence of other aspects of French
verse on him.   Modern poets certainly do not hold to the single-
verse theory.   No one, for example, who has examined the drafts
of almost any of the modern poems in the Poetry Collection of
the Lockwood Memorial Library (University of Buffalo) could
believe for one moment that a poet used the single-verse unit.
No less a poet-critic than Mr. Eliot reveals the weaknesses of
the single-verse unit.   "It seems to me," he said in the British
Academy Lecture on Milton (1947, pp. 12, 13), that Milton's verse
is especially refractory to yielding up its secrets to the examination of the single line.   For his verse is not formed in this way.
It is the period, the sentence, and still more the paragraph, that
is the unit of Milton's verse; and emphasis on the line structure
is the minimum necessary to provide a counter-pattern to the
period structure.   It is only in the period that the wave-length
of Milton's verse is to be found: it is his ability to give a perfect
and unique pattern to every paragraph, such that the full beauty
of the line is found in its context, and his ability to work in
larger musical units than any other poet—that is to me the most
conclusive evidence of Milton's supreme mastery.   The peculiar
feeling, almost a physical sensation of a breathless leap, com-
municated by Milton's long periods, and by this alone, is impossible to procure from rhymed verse.   Indeed, this mastery
is more conclusive evidence of his intellectual power, than is his
grasp of any *ideas* that he borrowed or invented.   To be able to
control so many words at once is the token of a mind of most
exceptional energy."   If we are to have a complete grasp of
Chaucer's achievement in the *Troilus* we need the entire stanza
rather than a two-verse unit.   That this is not an unusual point
of view is clear from its acceptance by the aesthetician, poet,
and poet-critic.[1]

The single-verse unit fails to give an accurate picture.   In
Chaucer, for example, hundreds of lines can be read as good iambic pentameters if we disregard the rhetorical sense;   they can
also be read to fit what we frequently speak of as the "rhetorical"
or "rhythmical" line, or what I think Chaucer and Lydgate
meant by verses of cadence.   An interesting illustration of the
confusion that arises from the use of the single-verse as a unit
is afforded by Mr. Alan Swallow's "The Pentameter Lines in

Skelton and Wyatt" (*MP*, XLVIII, 1-11) in which he attempts to show Skelton and Wyatt at the beginning of a movement toward a "full acceptance of the iambic pattern" rather than poets at the end of a tradition.   By confining himself to single lines, he deduces that most of them are "obviously" iambic; they need not, however, be so read, and to do so necessitates the abandonment of the tradition from Chaucer on.   Although Mr. Swallow is familiar with Mr. C. S. Lewis's "The Heroic Line in the Fifteenth Century", I am not certain that he grasps the full significance of some of Mr. Lewis's statements—at least he neither cites nor quotes what seem to me the important ones.

In his discussion of the heroic line, Mr. Lewis illustrates the importance of considering a line in its relation with those adjoining.   In the following the first line of stanza one is the final line of stanza two, but few readers would scan them in the same way.

> I have given no man of my fruit to eat
> I trod the grapes, I have drunken the wine.
> Had you eaten and drunken and found it sweet,
> This wild new growth of the corn and vine.

The first line determines the movement of the stanza, and I think most readers would scan it as follows:

$$\breve{}\ \breve{}\ |\ \acute{}\ \breve{}\ \breve{}\ |\ \acute{}\ \breve{}\ \breve{}\ |\ \acute{}\ \breve{}\ |\ \acute{}$$

although, quite possibly the initial *I* might have received a slight stress, ⸾.

In the following stanza, however, the first three verses control the movement of the final line:

> I comfort few and many I torment.
> Where one is spared a thousand more are spent;
> I have trodden many down beneath my feet,
> I have given no man of my fruit to eat.

If the reader pays careful attention I think he will read the final line as follows:

$$|\ \acute{}\ |\ \acute{}\ |\ \acute{}\ \breve{}\ |\ \acute{}\ |\ \acute{}\ \breve{}\ \breve{}\ |\ \acute{}\ \breve{}\ |\ \acute{}$$

Even if he employs the usual classical terms—certainly less subtle for English poetry than a musical notation—I think he would discover that he had read the first line as a four-stress one

made up of three anapests and an iamb; and the last as a five-
stress one with three trochees, an anapest, and an iamb. As
Mr. Lewis points out, as mere language they are identical. As parts
of different patterns, they assume different characteristics.
Incidentally, of course, since the conditions under which, according to the iambic hypothesis, final -e is sounded within the
verse in Chaucer never occur at the end, the multiple verse unit
is actually not necessary on purely linguistic grounds, important
though it be to an appreciation of the music of Chaucer's verse.

I have always been curious, however, to know how linguists
could justify the pronunciation of final -e in such examples as the
following, all of which are taken more or less at random from
Books I and II of the *Troilus*:

> And so bifel, whan comen was the time
> Of Aperil, when clothed is the mede
> With newe grene . . .
>
> —I, 155—157

> Of loves folk, lest fully the descente
> Of scorn fill on hymself;
>
> —I, 319, 320

> For for to trusten some wight is a preve
> Of truth, and forthi wolde I feyn remeve
> Thi wrong conseyte, and do the som wight triste
> Thi wo to telle; and tel me, if the liste.
>
> —I, 690—693

> And was the firste tyme he shuld hire preye
> Of love, O myghty God, what shul he seye ?
>
> —II, 1756, 1757

> But ofte gan the herte glade and quake
> Of Troilus, whil that he gan it rede
> So as the wordes gave hym hope or drede.
>
> —II, 1321—1323

> But natheles, when he had herd hym crye
> "Awake !'" he gan to syken wonder soore,
> And seyd . . .
>
> —I, 750, 752

> Swych his delit of foles to bywepe
> Hire wo, but seken bote they ne kepe.
>
> —I, 762, 763

> This Pandarus, tho desirous to serve
> His fulle frend, than seyd in this manere
>
> —I, 1068, 1059
>
> May I naught wel in other folk aspie
> Hire dredfull joye, hir constreinte, and hir peyne ?
>
> —II, 775, 776

There are at least 200 instances of the foregoing kind in Books I and II alone in which to pronounce the final -*e* is to break the normal prose rhythm. And if Chaucer would suppress a final -*e* at the caesura, why would he not do it at a stronger caesura at the end of a line ? The greatest weakness of the single-verse unit theory, however, is that it utterly neglects one of the main characteristics of poetry—its *rhythm*. Chaucer, being a good poet, realized that the rhythm of a passage was more important than such obvious ornaments as alliteration and rhyme. Less gifted writers tend to conceal their deficiency in the possession of rhythm by concentrating on these latter. The fault of Chaucer's followers is that they could not hear his rhythms except superficially. That was not because of the change in language but because of their aesthetic deficiencies. We must not lose sight of the structural unit simply because it has been vulgarized by a pedestrian poet like Lydgate, whose verses blunder and jingle toward the end of a structural unit (the hemistich) in a monotonous pattern that reveals the lack of a rhythmical and balanced structure. The single-verse myth, however, permitted the development of a more powerful myth— that of final -*e*.

(ii) *The Myth of the Final -E in Chaucer*
or
The Problem of Chaucer's Choice of Prosodic Basis

For Child, the myth of the single-verse unit was no myth. It was necessary to the formulation of his theory. It was imperative for the support of his hypothesis. Since it is Child's so-called "scientific" approach to language rather than the details of his results that is considered important, it is fitting that we look once more at his method. It is well known that the idea of the pronunciation of final unaccented -*e* in Chaucer was not recognized by the poets following Chaucer. Try to pronounce final -*e* in Hoccleve, Lydgate, or any of the other fifteenth-century poets and we have broken-backed lines. Spenser's imitation of Chaucer in the February eclogue ignores it, and the sixteenth-century editions of Chaucer's works disregard it. The idea was not even broached until Urry's edition of 1711 (published 1721), the period of greatest dominance of the heroic couplet tradition, when to be "correct" was the great desideratum. Certain "learned persons" had suggested to Urry that the final *e*'s were probably sounded. His edition, generally considered one of the worst from the point of view of actual text, reveals only too clearly that he had little understanding of historical grammar. Nothing more was done about final -*e* until Thomas Tyrwhitt suggested in 1775 that a possible model for Chaucer was the Italian *endecasillabo*, in which case final -*e* would be sounded. ("An Essay On the Language and Versification of Chaucer," in *Poetical Wks. of G. Ch.*, London, 1845, I, 146-251.)

Although a learned correspondent wrote that he could not "acquiesce in this notion" of Chaucer adopting the *endecasillabo*, Tyrwhitt gave his reasons for thinking his assumption correct. "When we reflect," he wrote, "that two of Chaucer's *juvenile productions*, the *Palamon and Arcite*, and the *Troilus*, were in a manner translated from the *Theseida* and the *Filostrato* of Boccacce, both written in the common Italian hendecasyllable verse, it cannot but appear extremely probable that his metre also was copied from the same original; and yet I cannot find that the form of his Stanza in the *Troilus*, consisting of seven verses was ever used by Boccacce, though it is to be met with among the poems of the King of Navarre and the Provençal Rimers." But Tyrwhitt was not dogmatic and concluded that either in Italian or French Chaucer would have found a number of models of correct and harmonious versification. Although Tyrwhitt's essay was steadily reprinted in the nineteenth century few paid any attention to his suggestions as to the pronunciation, possibly because of the able refutation of his position by G. F. Nott (*The Poet. Wks. of Wyatt and Surrey*, 1815). Child dismissed Nott in a high-handed manner and accepted Tyrwhitt's statement that Chaucer's model was the *endecasillabo*, and erected his elaborate structure on this doubtful hypothesis. "Of course," he wrote, "unless Chaucer wrote good metre, there is an end to all inquiry into the forms of his language. Nothing can be more absurd than Dr. Nott's theory upon this point . . . or more just than Tyrwhitt's remarks, which, however, did Nott no good" ("Observations on the Language of Chaucer", in *Memoirs of the American Academy of Arts and Sciences*, N.S VIII, Part I, 1861, pp. 449, 450 n.).   It was only after I had arrived independently at the basis of Chaucer's prosody which I shall propose that I read Nott and found that the bases were practically identical.   These were the same arrived at independently by Mr. C. S. Lewis in his study of Lydgate's verse. To write "good metre" is not, of course, the same as to write "correct" metre, as Child apparently thought.   When Child wrote his treatise he was still a young man fresh from two years' study of philology at one of the German universities.   The only reference to the basis for his method appears in the footnote that Tyrwhitt was right.   Now, what was Child's method ?

If a word occurred in rhyme in the MS, then the -*e* was pronounced.   That was proof enough.   Child realized, however, not every unaccented -*e* could be sounded, that elision occurred before a vowel or *h-*; although exceptions to this rule occurred on almost every page.   He assumed, too, that the *endecasillabo* was a line of regularly alternating stresses—an iambic pentameter line plus an unaccented syllable.   He overlooked Tyrwhitt's statement that the perfection of the *endecasillabo* had "never been determined, like that of our Heroic metre, to consist in the conformity of its accents to the pure Iambic measure" (n. 244).   Actually, of course, in practice even heroic metre has never strictly conformed to the iambic measure.   But Child, offering no proof for his hypothesis, confronted with exceptions on every page, and aware of strong disagreement of scholars, sets it up as a fact.   It is my contention, however, that this method is unscientific.   We are provided with no method for testing the end of the line, that part which is important for his hypothesis.   I suggested, therefore, that we should examine the conditions of the words within the line and from such an examination deduce whether or not the endecasyllabic theory was tenable.   Mr. Donaldson charged me with not taking into consideration the rules for elision other than before a vowel and h- —say, at the caesura, the vocative, and elsewhere.   But Child had expressly stated that -*e* final was sounded at the caesura under normal conditions when it would not be sounded elsewhere, and cited "on his schynë a mormal hadde he," "this was thyn othë—and myn eek certeyn," etc. (486). Mr. Donaldson also objected to many of the examples I used for my tests. In objecting he reveals a serious fallacy in his thinking. I was testing Child's assumptions on the basis of materials unavailable to Child—the extensive examples in the *Concordance*, but had, nevertheless, to work on Child's examples and assumptions. As we shall have occasion to see, Joseph Payne used the words in my essay to which Mr. Donaldson objected to prove that Child was in error in his deductions about final -*e* in rhyme. Because later investigators have rejected many of the words used by Child in his study, that does not mean that I could not use them. I *must* use them. We were testing Child's methodology. The fact that many of Child's examples have been ruled out is one more reason that his whole methodology should have been more carefully scrutinized. My count was, therefore, not only correct, but provided additional evidence in support of Payne who had approached the matter from the point of view of historical grammar. The probability for the non-pronunciation of final -*e* was therefore upheld. The two-verse unit would give another check. Quite obviously, I think, if the linguist is going to depend on metre to establish his theories, he must use it as it is employed by the poet. To set up his own restricted limits gives him but a partial truth. But so long as the investigator remembers that Child was working on a hypothesis and *not* on a proved fact, there is little danger.

Child's "Observations" was not received with unmixed acclaim. It is apparent that strong disagreement from many quarters, almost amounting to a rebellion, led him to protect himself when he continued his work on Gower. Instead of questioning the validity of his own method, however, he wrote: "It is entirely possible that further investigation may show that Chaucer is distinguished from Gower by the freer treatment of final -*e*, which occurring often, is to our ears so *puerile*, and which coming regularly at the end of each of a long succession of verses *produces a monotony all but intolerable*.[2] It is heartily to be hoped that this may be done, but in the meantime some signs of rebellion against the dominance of the offending letter make it necessary to repeat the suggestion already made in the paper on Chaucer, that we are not inquiring what sort of language and

verse is most agreeable but what was the actual rule of our
language at the end of the fourteenth century" ("Observations
on the Language of Gower's Confessio Amantis", Boston, 1868,
in Ellis, Part I—See footnote 12). It is quite possible that Child
would have rejected the current notion that Chaucer's language
differed from that of his contemporaries—that it was more
archaic. I think Skeat was responsible for this idea.

The support of F. J. Furnivall, secretary and founder of the
Chaucer Society, undoubtedly did much to make acceptable
Child's idea among those who were wavering; and many were.
In the *Temporary Preface to the Six-Text Edition* (London,
1868, pp. 1—3), Furnivall gave as an important reason for the
six-text edition the fact that since Morris's text had been printed
without his giving collation of such MSS as he had made,
Professor Child still pressed him "for a print of two or three
of the best MSS of the Canterbury Tales. He had produced in
the United States in 1862, *his masterly and exhaustive essay* on
the use of final -*e* in the Harleian MS 7334, as printed in M. T.
Wright's edition of the Canterbury Tales for the Percy Society
[a very inaccurate text]; and I felt that some return was due
to him from England for it." And, he added, "but when an
American who had done *the best bit of work on Chaucer's words*,
asked and kept on asking, for texts of our great English poet,
could an Englishman keep on refusing to produce them?"
especially, he adds, with complete irrelevance, when that young
man has done so much in the American Civil War against the
cause of slavery.

It is interesting to note that not only did Child include in his
critical apparatus means for showing what -*e*'s to add and which
to omit, but Furnivall defends his choice of MSS on the very
questionable assumption that the best MSS were the ones that
contained the most final -*e*'s. Although I anticipate, it is pertinent to remark that Furnivall, impressed by the attacks of the
able linguists, later reversed his position, and abandoned the
practice of sounding final -*e* in rhyme. He placed himself, he
said, "on the side of those sensible scribes who didn't sound the
-*e* at the end of the line in their own reading . . . and therefore
didn't write it" (Hoccleve, *Works*, 1892, III, xvii).[3] He chose
Harleian MS 4866 because "it had . . . fewer superfluous final
-*e*'s". The late Professor Gummere was another recalcitrant

who could not accept the pronunciation of final -*e* at the end of the line.

Child's essay elicited no outstanding response, although during the years following its publication, several articles appeared in the *Philological Society Transactions* on Chaucer's pronunciation, faulty rhymes, etc. The most important, by far, was the study, monumental in size and extent, useful if not always accurate, of A. J. Ellis (*On Early English Pronunciation*, with especial reference to Shakspere and Chaucer, 5 vols., 1867—1888). The material on final -*e* is in Part I, pp. 318—342. In this study Ellis included "a rearrangement of Child's 'Memoirs on the Language of Chaucer and Gower,'" but omitted to state the basis on which Child felt justified in adopting his methodology—that Tyrwhitt was right in thinking that Chaucer used the endeca-syllabic line. This was perhaps excusable since Child only mentioned it in a footnote (449). Ellis failed to realize that Child's elaborate study had been reared on an assumption, not a proved fact, and on a very tenuous assumption at that. He went one step farther than Child, however, in a very important matter. He did not discriminate between the final stressed -*e* and the final unstressed -*e*. "That -*e* final was at least occasionally pronounced," he wrote, "and that its sound did not differ, except in accent, from that of *me, the* . . . is conclusively proved by the following rhymes," and he cites *Rome, cynamome, sothe, youthe*, as rhyming with *to me*. Payne accepted this statement of Ellis. That Chaucer might have used them for conscious humorous effect did not occur to either.

Ellis attempted to strengthen the case for a sounded -*e* by himself analyzing the final -*e*'s within the lines. Mr. Donaldson accused me of believing that -*e*'s could be inserted at pleasure, which I certainly did not say, nor did I believe. It is possible that he thought I agreed with Gesenius who did maintain in his account of the language of Chaucer (1847) that Chaucer seemed "to add or omit final -*e* at pleasure, both in Anglo-Saxon and French words as was necessary to the metre" (III, 664). Ellis, who had given a condensed abstract of *De Lingua Chauceri* (pp. 87 ff.) undoubtedly had him in mind when he said a "Notion seems to have possessed some persons, that lines could be made to scan by omitting or inserting these -*e*'s at pleasure" (I, 320). Notice, however, that Ellis *assumed that a prosodic basis for*

Chaucer that scans regularly had been established, which, of course, it had not been. We have only Child's say-so. Ellis then analyzed the 23 cases from the first 100 lines in which the final -*e* was essential to the metre. These were Superfluous final -*e* (doubtful) 1; French final -*e*, 2; Essential final -*e*, 3; Verbal final -*e*, 6; Oblique final -*e*, 0; Adjectival final -*e*, 10; Adverbial final -*e*, 1. This examination revealed, he said, that the verbal and adjectival -*e*'s were the most important. He was making use, of course, of Child's deduction. He accepted as proved Child's statement that final -*e* was just beginning to disappear. It was Weymouth's contention that it had already disappeared. By accepting Child, Ellis could explain the pronunciation of final -*e* in certain positions. Although he rejected as absurd the insertion of -*e*'s at pleasure within the line, he condoned the idea when applied to the end: "Chaucer's verse seems to consist generally of five measures, with or without a final unaccented syllable, forming a 'feminine rhyme', added at the pleasure of the poet. There is no trace of the strict alternation of couplets with masculine and feminine rhymes which distinguishes French verse of the classical period" (I, 333). He says nothing about the French verse of Chaucer's period. No one would deny the presence of feminine rhymes in Chaucer, but to think of final -*e* as constituting a feminine rhyme especially when it had disappeared from the spoken language reveals little understanding of the genius of the English language.

Ellis laid far too much stress on the analogy of Chaucer's treatment of final -*e* with Goethe's practice in German. Tempting as it is to work on the analogy of foreign languages, those who have attempted to construct their arguments on analogies based on French, German, Dutch, Italian, Latin, etc.,—almost everything except English—are ranged one against the other. A scholar is sceptical of the value of such analogies as evidence. Not only are the investigators ranged one against the other, but when confronted with conflicting results based on the analogy of French and German versification, instead of admitting that the analogies are of little value, they temporize. Ellis found, for example, that, on the analogy of the French, "Chaucer *may* have used a final -*e* in poetry, which was unknown in common speech"; on the analogy of German where "final -*e* is a living part of the language and metre", and since "the foundation of our language is Saxon", it would seem more likely . . . that it was employed by English poets much in the same way now used by German poets" (I, 328, 329). This subtly leads him to an analysis of the first 100 lines of the Prologue, as I have already mentioned, where he found only 23 cases where the final -e was necessary to the metre. But what does Ellis do with such data ? He decides that would an editor of Chaucer "carefully examine all the final -e's, [restore] all those grammatically necessary, and ruthlessly [omit], or at least typographically [indicate], all those which neither grammar nor derivation allow, when they were not necessary for the metre or rhyme, and then submit the others to a careful consideration, he would do his study of English a great service" (I, 338, 339). And to what did this method lead Ellis ? To the conviction that "Chaucer and Goethe used the final -e in precisely the same way, with the exception of the consistent elision of -e before a vowel and silent h." Ellis was certainly ingenious, but scarcely scientific. He prepared the way for Skeat and Ten Brink, both of whom have done as much to retard the study of Chaucer's phonology as did Child.

The statistics quoted by Ellis from the Prologue (341) are misleading, because he assumes that for grammatical reasons the final -e in rhyme must still have been pronounced by Chaucer. This, we remember, was also the case with Kittredge, who specifically mentioned that his study on Chaucer's language *could not be used as a study in phonology* (G. L. Kittredge, "Observations on the Language of Chaucer's Troilus" (Harvard), *Studies and Notes in Philology and Literature* (1902), III, 389). When Kittredge began, he quite obviously thought that his study could be so used, else why should he provide such an elaborate phonetic machinery ?

The reader who will take the time to read Ellis's Chapter I, "On Pronunciation and Its Changes" or the early part of Chapter IV, "On the Pronunciation of English During the Fourteenth Century as Deduced from an Examination of the Rhymes in Chaucer and Gower" will realize the many questionable deductions he has made. Ellis, like most of these early investigators took a patronizing attitude toward Chaucer and his age, thinking of this period as naïve. We now know, of course, that no courts of Europe were more sophisticated than those of Edward III and his grandson Richard II, and the literacy of the upper classes of the fourteenth century has been ignored. As Mr. H. S. Bennet points out, "It cannot be too often stated that his writings were primarily for an educated and sophisticated audience, quick to take an allusion and well aware of the state of affairs which existed in political, social, or religious life (*Chaucer and the Fifteenth Century*, Oxford, 1947, p. 22). Mr. John Speirs (*Chaucer the Maker*, pp. 206, 207) points out that "Chaucer is no isolated genius. His poetry implies a cultivated audience and as such would lead us to expect that there were other cultivated poets among his contemporaries. It is what we do find—and I am not thinking only of Gower. Indeed, what we might scarcely be prepared for, even by the reading of Chaucer's remarkable various poetry, is the wealth and variety of the sophisticated poetry of his English contemporaries when we take the trouble to begin to investigate it as what it is— poetry. That it has been generally classified as unsophisticated and naïve is a reflection on the literary naïvete of modern scholarship." He further points out that Chaucer is the "end and climax of a social culture and a literary tradition, their fine flower—as well as the originator of later literary work," adding that "such poems as Chaucer's and Langland's, *Sir Gawayne and the Grene Knight*, and the Ballads with their conventions, their symbolic uses of language and various metrical systems and literary idioms, must have a long tradition—a history that needs disentangling and charting—of practice by poets and comprehension by audiences educated in responding to poetry". By not understanding this audience, Ellis was mistaken in or confused about the rate of change made by language from the fourteenth to the sixteenth centuries, a rapid change he thought largely the result of the Wars of the Roses.

With the acceptance of Child's views by Ellis, scholars who had previously remained silent, seeing that Child's theories were gaining acceptance, attempted to show the fallacies of Child's reasoning. The two important studies, studies which have been neglected by linguistic scholars, are Joseph Payne's "The Use of Final -e in Early English, with especial reference to the Final -e at the end of the verse in Chaucer's *Canterbury Tales*" (*Philol. Soc. Trans.*, 1868-69, pp. 86—153) and Richard Weymouth's "On *here* and *there* in Chaucer" (*Ibid.*, 1877-79, pp. 4—45).

Payne believed that whenever Chaucer pronounced final -*e*
it was a rhythmical licence (86). It is important to explain at
the outset, however, that Payne evidently assumed that Chaucer
employed an essentially iambic decasyllabic line; because he
believed that in words where the -*e* would normally be silent,
Chaucer would often pronounce it, as in "*smale* fowles" and
"*straunge* strondes", or in the definite adjective, as in "his *swete*
breeth", " The *yonge* sonne", etc. "On the whole," he concluded,
"in ordinary speech the definite -*e* was no longer pronounced,"
though Chaucer in his verse frequently used it as a "help to the
metre" (130). Payne stated that his purpose in writing the paper
would be to prove "that the -*e* of the final rhyme" in the *Canter-*
bury Tales was "not to be sounded" (135), and he said, he hoped
"to receive the thanks of Professor Child for disposing of thousands of cases of final -*e* at the end of the verse, which" he agreed
with him "in considering as a 'puerile sound', and as producing
by its constant recurrence at the end of a long succession of
verses 'a monotony all but intolerable' " (139, 140).

Although I believe Payne erred in thinking of Chaucer as
employing the iambic decasyllabic verse, and therefore pro-
nouncing -*e* within the verse for metrical reasons where I think
it should be silent, his methodology is sound from the point of
view of historical grammar, which Child's was not. He believed
that the introduction of Norman speech into England and the
usages of the Norman scribes were the cause of the gradual
disappearance of final -*e* in the twelfth century. The Norman
dialect was, he said, "the simplest and purest of all dialects of
the French language, and largely exhibited the influence of
phonetic laws" (87). Anglo-Norman affected the English
orthography by "introducing an expedient of the Norman scribes
(before unknown in England), which consisted in the addition
of an inorganic -*e* to denote the length of the radical vowel".
He cited as examples, A.S. *lár, bén, béd* into *lare, bene, bede*.
This -*e* was never sounded. I think modern scholars agree with
Payne. We must remember, however, that Child had used these
words as examples of where the -*e* *was* sounded.

Payne dismissed Ellis's statement "that Chaucer and Goethe
used the final -*e* in precisely the same way" ("On Early English
Pronunciation", 339) and Child's "that the unaccented final -*e*
of nouns of French origin is sounded in Chaucer as it is in French

verse" ("Observations", 461) because "the use of -*e* in German and French versification is . . . regular and constant, while that in Chaucer is constantly interfered with by instances of silent -*e*. . . ." (88, 89). Elsewhere, I have expressed a similar opinion arrived at independently.

Child maintained that -*e* was sounded at the caesura when it would otherwise be silent. Payne disagreed with Child, and maintained that -*e* was silent at the "prosodial bars". Incidentally, all later scholars have agreed with Payne, although credit is generally given to Schipper. Payne did not err in thinking of the virgule as a caesura; his term was "prosodial bars". Before he formulated what he felt to be the practice of the English poets, he quoted Quicherat, *Versification française* (325): "Une preuve de l'importance que nos anciens poétes donnaient au repos de la césure" (he means sectional pause) "c'est qu'ils la traitaient comme la rime, et lui permettaient de prendre une syllabe muette, qui n'etait pas compté dans la mesure" (91). This principle, in its application to Anglo-Norman and English could be formulated as follows: "The -*e* that occurred at the sectional pause (and, presumptively, that at the final pause closing the verse) was silent, and not a factor of the rhythm" (91). He then cited examples from the *Chanson de Roland*, Deschamps, and Rutebeuf; from De Brunne, Handlyng Synne, William of Palerne; and finally from Chaucer. From these examples, he assumed that the -*e* was silent at the "greater pause, that formed by the end of the verse" (93). This last assumption has not, of course, been accepted by many linguists.

Payne did not rest his case on the foregoing reasoning. In fact, his main arguments were yet to follow. He then set up his "Canons of orthography and orthoepy", which he attempted to prove. It is not feasible to review here all of his arguments. It is sufficient to state that the classes of words which he shows to have a silent -*e* were the same words that Child listed as proof that -*e* was sounded. However scholarly Child later became, Payne far surpassed him in his methodology of the solution of the problem of -*e*. Incidentally, also, many of the words used by Mr. Donaldson to show that I erred in using words where the -*e* had never been sounded, were first demonstrated to be such by Payne. But, as I pointed out, I was testing Child. Payne showed by reference to the Ormulum that Child was wrong in using A.S. monosyllables as examples where -*e* was sounded, He showed, too, that Child was deficient in his knowledge of Anglo-Norman. "The Norman words like *place, grace, face, space*" as "interpreted in English by *plas, graas, faas, spas*" were, said Payne, "found in 'Early English Poems', and later in Chaucer." Conversely he found *trespace, case* for the French *trespas, cas*; and "both in Early French and English . . . equivalent forms, *devis, devise,* and *device; servis, servise, service*" etc. In an earlier paper in the *Philol. Soc. Transactions* for 1869-70, (pp. 371, 418-19, 440), Payne had shown the phonetic identity of -s, -sse, -ce, in Anglo-Norman and English. Continuing with his discussion, he showed that in words like *dame, fame,* and *schame* the -*e* was silent, and then to words in -eme *dreme,* -ime *rime,* -ome *dome,* -ume *coustume,* -ene *quene,* -ine *pine,* as well as -ede *bede,* -ete *swete,* -ote *note,* -ut *prute,* -ere *chere,* etc. (100, 101). Because of restrictions of space he considered words in -are, -ere, -ire, -ure, -age, -ance, as types of the class.

Because of a persistent misconception among many modern scholars about words in -ere, -ire, etc., let us examine these words more closely. Child had asserted that "there can be no doubt that -*e* final was generally pronounced after r," which, said Payne, was "a conclusion inconsistent with the law of formation already considered, and, as it would appear, with general usage in early Anglo-Norman and English" (101). Words in -are, -ere, -ire, -ore, were, he said, "monosyllables in the thirteenth century. It [was], therefore, extremely improbable that these words would in the fourteenth century put on another syllable. And if not these words, why others of the same termination as *deere* and *cheere* ?" (101). The following example from "A Sarmun" (98) are a few of those used to show that Child was wrong:

Boþe *fire* (A.S. fýr) and wind lude sul crie   v. 125

To crie ihsu þin *ore* (A.S. ár)   v. 142

While þou ert *here* (A.S. hér) be wel *iware* (A.S. gewár)

    v. 143

Undo þin hert and live is *lore* (A.S. lár)   v. 144

Payne believed, moreover, that Ellis was in error when, in quoting from Wright's edition of Chaucer [a very inaccurate text], he maintained that the spelling indicated "a difference of pronunciation" and that, accordingly many of Chaucer's rhymes were faulty. As examples, Ellis listed "(1) *trace, allas,* (1953); *solace, allas* (9149); (2) *bere, messager* (5142); *ever, dissevere* (12802); *mater, gramer* (14946); (3) *hew, newe* (8253); *may, aye* (17105); *leye, pray, way* (8753),—in which, if the assumption is correct, we certainly have a collection of 'faulty rhymes'. But then, that is the question at issue," and, said Payne, Ellis offered no proof that *solace* should be three syllables. This failure to offer proof, we must remember, was also Child's method. It was Payne's contention, and modern scholars agree with him, that such examples as Ellis listed were, in fact, good "ear" rhymes, although not good "eye" rhymes.

Contrary to Payne's expectations, however, Child did not thank him for disposing of the thousands of final -*e*'s in rhyme. Instead, Child's very close friend, James Russell Lowell, mis-represented Payne's entire argument in *My Study Windows*. It is difficult to understand the asperity with which Lowell attacked Payne (without mentioning him by name), or how he could deliberately misrepresent Payne's contentions. Lowell's attack was probably made out of consideration for Child rather than from deliberate dishonesty; but in any case it is inexcus-able. Lowell charged Payne with having "undertaken to prove that Chaucer did not sound the final or medial -*e*," and to throw "us back on the old theory of 'riding-rhyme', that is, verse to the eye and not to the ear". Payne defended himself in an Appendix to his essay when it was finally printed in volume form, first chiding Lowell for "a certain 'Sir Oracle' air, which scarcely befits a Professor of the Humanities." He admitted that Chaucer sounded the -*e* for metrical reasons, maintained that his position was contrary to Lowell's statement that Chaucer wrote "verse to the eye and not to the ear" (152), and revealed Lowell's ignorance of Anglo-Norman writers. Lowell, said Payne, had drawn his examples from the usage of standard French, and was therefore irrelevant (153).[4] Mr. Lowell was, notwithstanding, said Payne, "a charming writer, and if he did not profess to know everything, and were not so very positive in his assertions, would be more charming still" (153). The statement "verse to the eye and not to the ear" is interesting in that it shows the almost complete dominance of the iambic decasyllable in the latter part of the nineteenth century. Payne never mentioned Nott. In all probability, none of these scholars would have considered our modern rhythmical line, however regular, as verse.

Skeat, ignoring Payne, undoubtedly did much toward the acceptance of Ellis's views (Thomas Chatterton, *Poetical Works*, with an essay on the Rowley Poems by the Rev. Walter Skeat, London, 1871, XII, xiii). "Our knowledge of the pronunciation of early English," he wrote, "is still uncertain, but more advance has at length been made, and the whole problem has been resolutely, and ably handled in the masterly work on *Early English Pronunciation* by Mr. Alexander J. Ellis. Professor Child has thoroughly examined the rimes employed by Chaucer, and tests have even been deduced by means of which the probable genuineness of some of the works ascribed to him may be examined."

Not all scholars accepted Ellis's findings in preference to those of Payne. Richard Weymouth ("On Early English Pronunciation, with especial reference to Chaucer—in Opposition to the Views Maintained by Mr. A. J. Ellis", London, 1874, p. 1) may be considered their spokesman. He attacked Ellis's premises and expanded his views into book form four years later. Since this essay has seemingly been overlooked or forgotten, some of his charges may be briefly reviewed. It is interesting that later scholars have often justified Weymouth's views by adopting them without acknowledgment. Weymouth accuses Ellis of confusing languages proper, the *living voice*, with symbols on black paper, believing that a study of dialects would throw important light on the actual pronunciation. Incidentally, Ellis later did this, publishing his findings in Part V of his "On Early Pronunciation" (1889). Weymouth believed that Chaucer's language was much closer to that of Shakespeare than not. He not only did not believe the final -*e* was sounded, but also disagreed markedly from the vowel sounds put forward by Ellis. He did not believe that Ellis was realistic in thinking that the Wars of the Roses had made a decided break in the development of the language. It was not Mr. Ellis's industry, but his logic and the general conduct of his argument that he objected to. Three years later, in his "On *here* and *there* in Chaucer," he discussed Ellis's over-simplification of his treatment of the vowel sounds. The details of this article will be more profitably reviewed when we consider the myth arising from the greater one of the pronunciation of final -*e*—the myth that Chaucer never rhymed words in -*er* with those in -*ere*.

Gradually, scholars were inclined to shift from the Italian *endecasillabo* to the French decasyllable of Central French as the basis. But what should they do about the pronunciation of final -*e* at the end of the line ? They created myths. In the statements that Chaucer (1) followed the French practice of mute -*e*, (2) was identical with Goethe's practice of elision, and (3) never rhymed words in -*er* with those in -*ere*, we have three myths still accepted by many linguists, and in arguments, often more heated than logical, I have been confronted with each one, often with all together although they might be mutually contradictory. Before considering Schipper's *Altenglische Metrik* (1881), the first detailed study of Chaucer's prosody, let us dispose of these myths.

ii.—(a) The Myth of French Mute -E in Chaucer

French mute -*e* is, we know, sounded in music. But is it sounded in reading, or is its effect essentially that of heightening the quality of the preceding vowel and intensifying the consonant ? That it served the latter purpose was the statement of a friend of mine who had studied at La Comedie Française. She is supported by the authority of French prosodists—M. de Banville (*Petit Traité de Poesie Française*), Arthur Gosset (*A Manual of French Prosody*, London, 1884), and others. Gosset, in reality quoting from de Banville, says the following: "The mute syllable at the end of a feminine line is *not* pronounced in reading, reciting, or acting, save in so far as a *very* faint sound may be necessary to bring out the full pronunciation of the consonants (if any) supporting it. Thus, with such a feminine termination as *ombre* or *astre*, the final -*e mute* is a little more audible than with the endings *ite* or *ée*" (927). This is a very different thing from making the English unaccented -*e* into a distinct syllable as the early grammarians would have done. But even if it were sounded in French would Chaucer adopt as his practice so un-English a custom, and one that would distort the rhythms of English speech ? As the late Professor Raleigh wrote in *On Writers and Writing* (Quoted in Speirs, pp. 18, 19): "His style is the perfect courtly style; it has all the qualities of

ease, directness, simplicity, of the best colloquial English. . . .
He avoids all 'counterfeited terms', all subtleties of rhetoric and
addresses himself to the 'commune intente'. . . . Now a style
like this, and in this perfection, implies a society at the back
of it. If we are told that educated people at the Court of
Edward III spoke French and that English was a despised
tongue, we could deny it on the evidence of Chaucer alone. His
language was not shaped by rustics. No English style draws
so much as Chaucer's from communal and colloquial elements of
the language. And his poems make it certain that from his
youth up he had heard much admirable witty talk in the English
tongue." The idea that Chaucer would adopt one pronunciation
for his prose and a more archaic one for his poetry reveals what
happens when a person not well-versed in poetry attempts to
use what he does not understand.

ii.—(b) *The Myth of the Analogy between Chaucer's and Goethe's
Practice*

Little need be said about this myth. At the time Goethe wrote
unaccented final -e had not disappeared, nor was it in the process
of disappearing; nor is it now. His use of elision was purely
a poetic practice and is so regarded by educated Germans. In
the English of Chaucer's day, final -e had already passed out
of use.

ii.—(c) *The Myth of Chaucer's Not Rhyming Words in -er and -ere*

More important is the myth that Chaucer never rhymes words
in -*er* with those in -*ere*. Although such statements were based
on the evidence of certain scribal practices—and often on inaccurate transcripts of MSS—what are the facts ? One well-
known linguist has assured me that could I disprove this myth
every linguist must be convinced and abandon the pronunciation
of final -e. When I reminded him that it had already been done,
he began to find excuses. Linguistic scholars have neglected,
I think, one of the finest linguists of the period—Richard
Weymouth. Had they heeded him the course of linguistic
studies during the past seventy years might well have been
different. Certainly a tremendous amount of useless effort could
have been avoided. What is the testimony of Chaucer's rhymes;
what, for example, can we learn from a study of Chaucer's *here*

and *there* ? Why do we not, ask the linguists, find words in *-er* rhyming with words in *-ere*. Actually, we do find such rhymes. Weymouth, adopting a logical method that withstands the most careful scrutiny, showed that Ellis had failed to grasp the true situation and was oversimplifying—and thereby falsifying—the facts. Actually this study by Weymouth was a "reconstruction and expansion of the argument" which he had presented to the Philological Society, read in 1870, and subsequently enlarged into a thin octavo published independently of the Society. In this octavo of 1874, he had stated that a true picture of Chaucer's practice could be obtained only by a study of the living language, particularly of the dialects. He did not believe the scribes' use of final *-e* in their writing was important. He did believe, however, that the same symbols often represented several different sounds. Ellis, as I have mentioned, acted upon this statement of Weymouth, but in Weymouth's opinion, over-simplified the matter. In his criticism of Ellis, Weymouth supported his arguments with the data gathered from a careful examination of 1246 rhymes of words ending in *-ere* or *-er* or *-eere* or *-eer*. ("The final *-e*" he wrote, "I may say once for all, I have not taken into account. I have had quite work enough on hand without it" (312). He knew that it was what the word meant and not how it was spelt that was important.) Weymouth's suggestions are those which underlie most of the studies in ME phonology which relate it to NE phonology. The results of his investigations are interesting. The word *here*, he says, "has four distinct meanings: it may be (*a*) the verb *hear*, or (*b*) the adverb *here*, or (*c*) the noun *hair*, or (*d*) the personal pronoun *her*. If it bears either of the first two meanings, it rhymes in *all* our Early English poets with *dere*, adj., *dere*, s., *clere*, *chere*, etc., and only very rarely and exceptionally with *were* from *be*, *where*, *there*, *swere*, vb., *forbere*, etc. But it is with these latter words that it rhymes in either the third or fourth sense, and rarely or never with the former." He then considers briefly the case of *were*: "So *were* has seven different meanings: it may be (*a*) the plural of *was*, it may be (*b*) the past subjunctive of the same verb, it may be (*c*) the modern verb *wear*, or (*d*) the now obsolete *were* = protect, it may mean (*e*) war, or (*f*) husband, or (*g*) doubt or perplexity. In the first six of these senses it rhymes with *there* and its class; in the last sense only does it rhyme with *deere, cleere,* etc., and it rhymes with these—with only two exceptions that I have discovered anywhere—not only in Chaucer but in Lyndesay's Poems . . ., in Handlyng Synne, in Robert of Brunne's Chronicle, and in short in the whole of our early English poetry. From this it is evident that we have two distinct classes of words in -*ere* in Early, as in Modern, English, of which two adverbs [now pronounced as in *here* and *there*] may be taken as types respectively" (320, 321). This essay also appears in *Essays on Chaucer,* 2nd series, IV (1878), 311—353, and it is to this essay that my page numbers refer).

Weymouth also examined words ending in -*eke,* -*ene,* -*ete,* etc., and found that "neither of these classes (except very rarely words of the second class) will rhyme with *sette, bedde, henne,* and other such words with the short *e.*" The obvious conclusion was that "there were in the fourteenth century three different sounds represented by one and the same symbol, just as at present" (321). Not content with his examination of the sounds in English, he approached his thesis from several points of view, the results of which he summarizes on pp. 352 and 353. I cannot overstress the fact that Weymouth's approach to Chaucer's language was from the point of view of the *sounds represented by the symbols* and not from that of the symbols themselves; whereas the symbols, or *schriftsprache* of the scribes, were the concern of the German grammarians.

Weymouth believed strongly in the stability of the English dialects which "have remained in a great degree unchanged for centuries, till the ponderous roller of national education comes in our time to level all distinctions in modes of speech." He found untenable the notion that the Wars of the Roses would occasion a vast change in the mode of speech of the whole nation, and remarked of Ellis's belief that the Wars had been responsible, "never did Queen Mab spin a flimsier cobweb in the brain of any man" (323). I think most scholars agree with Weymouth. In his edition of Grosseteste's *Castel off Love* (*Phil. Soc. Trans.,* 1865, p. 9), he shows an attitude toward the language of this MS of about 1370, which he believed to be the language of "the beginning of the fourteenth century" which is far from dogmatic and is certainly more scholarly than that of Child, Ten Brink, Skeat, and other early editors of the text of Chaucer. "I have," he writes, "nowhere either added or cut off a final *e*; not even, by any kind of accent, marked such an *e* as necessarily sounded. My theory is that whenever the final *e* represents a final syllable in Anglo-Saxon, it *may*—not *must*—be sounded; and never otherwise." His notes on lines 32, 331, 830, and his glossarial comments on *drihte, boþe*, and *wiþoute* throw valuable light on his attitude.[5]

Just as Chaucer was careful to avoid rhyming words which would now be all right, so did he rhyme words in which the vowels have changed so that the rhyme would no longer be possible. The obvious example of this is his rhyming to *seke, inf.*, seek, with *seke, adj.*, sick. It would be dangerous to assume that merely because the unaccented -*e* had ceased being pronounced, the quality of the root vowel had suddenly altered. Changes do not take place so quickly. Professor Helge Kökeritz (*A Guide to Chaucer's Pronunciation*, mimeograph, p. 8) by following Weymouth's strictures—consciously or unconsciously —of working on the living language has demonstrated the truth of Weymouth's arguments.

In the foregoing pages we have examined some of the myths affecting phonology. It is now important to see how these myths inspired larger myths of prosody.

CHAPTER THREE

THE MYTHS OF THE FOREIGN SOURCES FOR CHAUCER'S PROSODY

THE first extensive study of Chaucer's prosody was that of Jakob Schipper (*Altenglische Metrik*, 1881). He acknowledged his debt to Skeat, Ellis, and particularly to Child, because the latter had provided the basis for the pronunciation of Chaucer in his "bewunderswürdigen Werke On Early English Pronunciation" (436). He ignored Weymouth. Instead of assuming that the English "five-stress" line was built on the endecasyllabic, he assumed that it was built on the French. Notice, however, the fallacy in his reasoning—the type of fallacy which we find so frequently in these early investigators. By abandoning the basis for Child's deduction of the pronunciation of final -*e*, he should have realized that he could not retain Child's results. Child made his deductions on one assumption; Schipper made his on the basis of another, but retained the results of a hypothesis he abandoned. Logic, it becomes all too evident as one reviews these early works, is not a strong characteristic of their Teutonic methodology. It is not necessary to review here all of Schipper's hypotheses, except to say that he believed English poetry was derived from the French, that this had a rising rhythm, with the caesura generally after the fourth syllable. He did recognize, however, that Chaucer used a varying caesura. Schipper lacked any sense whatever of the historical processes. He applied to Chaucer's verse of the fourteenth century, for example, rules for French verse that came in with Ronsard and Du Bellay in the sixteenth. It is also clear that Schipper mistook the virgule (/) for a caesural rather than a rhetorical mark. But of this, more later.

Bernhard Ten Brink (*Chaucers Sprache and Verskunst*, 1884), acknowledging his debt to Tyrwhitt, Gesenius, Child, Ellis, and Schipper, assumes a more dogmatic tone about Chaucer's prosody than we have yet encountered. His editorial methods, shocking to a modern scholar, involved extended emendation. "It goes without saying," he wrote, "that MS forms which the evidence of rime and metre proves to be incompatible with Chaucer's phonetic system have been removed and replaced by more appropriate ones" and he insisted "upon the applications of certain principles of a normalized orthography" (English translation, p. 33). He would not tolerate anapestic or trochaic rhythms (§ 300, p. 209), and where they occurred he would emend the text. It should be obvious by now to any reader not suffering from a blocked mind that Chaucer's phonetic system has not been established by those scholars looked upon by Ten Brink as his authorities. The scholars who were scientific in their methodology were ignored.

In the preface to the English translation (1910), Schipper bases his study of final -e on Ten Brink's *Chaucers Sprache and Verskunst*, a curious case of indebtedness in a circle.

Ten Brink marks the extreme position towards Chaucer's verse—a strongly iambic verse with no permitted trochaic or anapestic substitutions, with the caesura after the fourth syllable. And Ten Brink's position is the one still held by a great many linguists. Professor Kökeritz (*A Guide to Chaucer's Pronunciation*) speaks of Chaucer's regularly alternating stresses, and Mr. H. Talbot Donaldson several times mentions his adherence to a rather stricter iambic verse than many investigators allow.

It will be necessary, of course, to review the tenableness of the endecasyllabic and iambic decasyllabic bases in some detail. Before doing so, however, what were the results of these studies in Teutonic methodology ? The texts issued by the Chaucer Society were edited from the point of view of the decasyllabic theory, spelling was regularized, final *e*'s were inserted where metrically necessary, and instead of order being introduced, chaos took over and the entire fifteenth century became arraigned as metrically incompetent.

But changes were in the wind and fancy was slowly giving way to fact. The German investigators continued, however, to investigate the *Schriftsprache* rather than Chaucer's actual speech. Lorenz Morsbach (*Mittelenglische Grammatik*, 1896) recognized that *final* e *had become silent generally by the middle of the fourteenth century*, but thought it was still pronounced in rhyme. He quoted Ten Brink as his authority (Anm. 1, p. 112). I believe Morsbach was correct in his general deduction but not in the matter of Chaucer's pronunciation of *e* in rhyme. Joseph Frieshammer (*Die Sprachliche Form der Chaucerschen Prosa*,

Halle, 1910) showed the influence of Morsbach and Ten Brink. He supports Morsbach in his deduction that unaccented *e* was silent in prose, listing *bliss* as the usual form in Chaucer's prose; he defers to Ten Brink, however, by pointing out that "auch einmal im Reim" it was *blisse: kisse* (10). What he could not know at that time was that in the Merthyr fragment (4389), the oldest MS of Chaucer, we have *blys* without the *e*.[6] One of the defects of these investigators, however, was, as I have mentioned before, that they all, like Child, Ellis, and others, confused the *written speech* with the *spoken speech* and Chaucer's spelling with that of the scribes. Weymouth called attention to the first danger, and Manly has much to say on the second.

Manly points out (I, 558) that the scribes (not monks as was once thought) "were taught in schools or trained in shops, and that they inevitably formed habits in spelling as in writing" and that "good professional scribes by training wrote and spelled well". This statement supports Weymouth's that the scribes' use of final -*e* was not important. Since we have no MS in Chaucer's hand, it is unlikely that any of the MSS represent his spelling. It is interesting to note, however, that the oldest known MS, the Merthyr, dating from about 1400, reveals "no signs of supervision, no corrections, but [is] certainly the work of a professional scribe". This MS is in the East Midland dialect, shows the loss of many final -*e*'s (*sklender, never, shent, had, thilk, blyth, both, mery, said,* etc.), and the presence of some scribal *e*'s and some forms out of the ordinary (*keen—kine, height—highte, flaugh—flew, hundreth*), as well as a few spellings that occur more often in late than in early MSS (I, 362). Although the spellings of the MSS having the best texts agree in general, "it is not wise to conclude," according to Manly, "as has sometimes been suggested (cf. Macaulay's introduction to the *Confessio Amantis*, and Root's *Troilus*), that . . . these MSS reproduce the spelling of the original. It is far more likely that the agreement means that they were made by scribes who had received the same type of training" (I, 560).

Modern studies of Chaucer's prosody have been hampered by the inability of the investigators to free themselves from the tyranny of certain ideas of phonology based on the foregoing myths that have never been proved. Although Sir George Young adheres to certain myths, he rejects Ten Brink's treatment of stress shift (§274)—(1) that the accent must yield to the demands of the verse, or (3) the use of level stress, "a contradiction in terms"—and finds the only phase admissible the one dismissed by Ten Brink as superfluous (31, 31)—(2) that "the rhythm must conform to the normal accentuation: inversion of the metrical measure" (English translation, 1901, §274).

What is characteristic of Sir George Young is even more characteristic of an earlier investigator, Albert H. Licklider (*Chapters on the Metric of Chaucerian Tradition*, 1907). He begins promisingly, showing the misjudgements by many critics, but he soon bogs down. Like Mr. Swallow, he prefers to think of Chaucer as the father of the modern heroic line (Ten Brink's contention), with its allowable variations. Again, it is quite obvious that the concept of the pronunciation of final *e* was the deterring factor.

Before I begin to construct what I believe is the prosodic basis for the verse used by Chaucer in the *Troilus* and the *Canterbury Tales*—what Chaucer himself called verses of cadence—we must examine the tenableness of the prosodic theories adopted by linguistic investigators.

Although the endecasyllabic theory as a basis for Chaucer's prosody has been generally discarded, the fact that it is the basis for the pronunciation of final -*e* necessitates some consideration of it. Actually, of course, it is the vestigial remains of this theory that are responsible for the idea that the pronunciation of Chaucer's poetry is more archaic than his prose, an assumption which I cannot accept because it is contrary to the practice of every known good poet. A poet may use, as did Spenser, an archaic vocabulary, but he cannot use an archaic pronunciation. I believe that scholars agree not only that final -*e* in Chaucer's prose was not sounded, but that it had ceased being pronounced in London English. We have the subjective evidence of English prose rhythms to show that it was not sounded, in addition to scribal evidence of *e*'s omitted from prose that are present in Chaucerian MSS. Three of the examples I have chosen are from documents collected by Chambers and Daunt (*London English*, 1384—1425, Oxford, 1931), the fourth from a sermon, and the fifth from the personal letters written by Lady Zouche who was, as Miss Rickert has pointed out ("Some English Personal Letters of 1402", *RES*, VIII, 257—83), probably of Chaucer's circle with a knowledge of his work.   The first selection is from *Gilda Carpenter London* (1389):

"Also is ordeined þat uche brother and soster of þis fraternite schal paie to þe helpyng and susteyning of seke men, which þat falle is dissesse, as by falling down of an hous, or hurtyng of an ax, or oþer diuerse sekenesses, twilfe penyes by þe yer" (42).

The second is from the Testamentum Roberti Aueray (1411):

"I, Robert Aueray: Ferst y by-queþe my soule to god and to our lady, and to All the companye of heven, and my body to ben y-beryed in the church of seynt clementis wyth-owtyn Templebarr at london.   Also y be queþe to the werk of the same church xij d" (216).

The third appears in Presentment By a Jury (1396—1397):

"And also the friday folwynge in þe same Woke of Estarne, in þe same ȝer of owre lord the kyng XVJᵉ, Thomas Bradle, John Spalding, Wylliam Schyngilwode, preest and Richard langeford, with other moe une-knowen, in þe feld of Steben-ythe, up-on þe land of John ȝereld by-syde Schordych, with force and armes, bowes and arwes, swerdes and bokelers & other wepene, a þere asawt madyn to þe sone of John ȝereld and to þe ȝomen of Schordych, þat þere were in amendyng of here berseles, her boweȝ & her schoveleȝ brokyn and hewen, & hem foule afrayeden, þat þei dredyn hem of her lyues, ageynns þe kynges pees" (234).

The fourth is from a sermon preached at St. Paul's Cross, London, on Quinquagesima Sunday, 1388 (Göteborgs Högskolas Årsskrift, XXXI, 11, 1925).   The rhythms are modern in feeling:

"... ryȝt so in þe chyrche þre officirs ben nedeful: preesthede, knythed, *and* laborerys.   to *p*restys it falliþ to kytte a way þe voide braunches of synnys with þe sworde of her tonge. to kiȝttys it falliþ to let wroggys and þeftys to be don, *and* to maytyn godd*ys* lave *and* oþir lond*ys*, and to laborerys it to falliþ to *t*raveyl bodily *and with* her sore sotte to gete out of þe erþe her bodily lif lode for *hem and* for oþir partyis. *and* þeise stat*ys* ben also so nedeful to þe chirche þat non may wil byn *with* outy*n* oþir ..." (2).

The fifth contains phrases which, to quote Miss Rickert, "suffice to show that the spoken English of Chaucer's time was not so unlike our own":

> was at home with me at Eytoun and so I spake to him of Broke
> let put them all together in the great coffer and send them
>   home to Eytoun
> more than it is ten times worth
> and but ye may get the same man that ye spoke to me of
> send me two yards of the breadth that is marked here
> but great wages and dispenses he axeth for his being there
> I would a prayed you that ye would have ordained me a pair
>   of beads of gold for my lady my mother
> send me word what price of an whole cloth of black velvet

Any system of prosody that radically departs from the foregoing prose rhythms of the London dialect—rhythms which are similar to those of Chaucer's prose—is suspect. The rhythm of the lines from Lady Zouche's letters is not so different from the following excerpts taken at random from Book II of the *Troilus*:

> I have so grete a pyne for love   1165/6
> Ne make hire selven bonde in love   1223/4
> it were ek to soone to graunten hym so grete a libertee 1290/1
> whan that it was eve, and al was wel   1302/3
> Gan to desiren moore than he did erst   1339/40
> for to bygynne to han a manere routhe   1374/5
> and torn we anon to Pandarus, that gan ful faste prye
>   that al was wel   1709/11

I have purposely refrained from indicating the line divisions in the foregoing because the normal prose rhythms would be destroyed when read according to the generally accepted reading of Chaucer's verse, particularly of sounding final -*e* in rhyme.

Professor Kökeritz (*Ibid.*, 2) also points out that "in colloquial language of the period, final unstressed *e* was dying fast". What could be more colloquial than most of the conversation in the *Troilus*? He believes, however, that Chaucer uses it as "an important metrical device." There is little indication that he understands what Chaucer's metre actually was.

(i) *The Endecasyllabic Myth*

Since modern studies stem from Child's "Observations on the Language of Chaucer", and since Child accepted without ques-

tion Tyrwhitt's suggestion that possibly Chaucer might have
adopted the endecasyllabic, we must examine the tenableness
of Child's position. This unsupported blanket acceptance on
the part of Child seems incredible, especially since he had a
mathematical background, and so should have had some understanding of the logical processes. But did he even understand
the nature of the Italian *endecasillabo* ? Did he understand the
great flexibility of this form, and, despite its origins, its essentially non-metrical but rhythmical quality ? And its great
flexibility from the point of view of placing the accent was
undoubtedly the reason it appealed to Dante and Boccaccio.
We must remember, however, as Kittredge has warned us, that
the study of Middle English philology was only in its beginnings
when Child began his study. He had studied philosophy,
classics, and Germanic philology at Göttingen and Berlin from
1849-51, at the age of twenty-six, was granted his Ph.D. (Göttingen) in 1854, and published his "Observations" in 1863. The
average aspirant for a Ph.D. today has a sounder knowledge of
Germanic philology than was possible in Child's day.

Unfortunately, I have found no treatment of the *endecasillabo*
in English, but Attilio Levi (*Della Versificazione*, Genoa, 1931)
and Pasquale Leonetti (*Storia Della Tecnica Del Verso Italiano*,
Parte Prima, Milan, 1933) point out certain qualities that would
have appealed to Chaucer—qualities which he could find in both
French and English prosody of his day. After an exhaustive
treatment of the *endecasillabo* (57—66), Signior Levi summarizes
his findings: "Ricapitolando, tre sono le formule dell' endecasillabo: settenario + quinario, quinario + settenario, quinario
+ senario. Ma naturalment, sono possibili tutte quante le
forme, cioè le 30 del settenario, le 12 del quinario, le 9 del senario.
Quindi, traducendo in cifre le formale anzidelle, si hanno
30 × 12 = 360, 12 × 30 = 360, 12 × 9 = 108, e, sommando
i prodotti (360 + 360 + 108) si perviene ad 828, che rappresenta
(se i mili calcoli sone esatti) il numero stragrande della combinaz-
ioni, di cui e suscettibile l'endecasillabo" (66).

Signior Leonetti explains the origin of the rhythmic variations
of the *endecasillabo*: "Senza dilungarni in considerazioni analoghe
per gli altri due giambi interne, ritengo per ora sufficiente aver
fissato il principio che tutte le variazioni ritmiche dell' endecasillabo si dipartono da una pentapodia primitiva in seguito ai

due fatti dello spostamento e della perdita d'accento dei prima quatro giambi, e particularmente dei tre interni. Il medesimo principio può valere per gli altri versi dallo schema fondamentale giambico e per l'ottonario dallo schema fondamentale trocaico, e può dispensare non solo dall' applicare ai versi italiani l'ingegnosa teoria del Fraccaroli propria dei metri latini, ma anche dal ricorrere a nuove sistemazioni ritmiche, quali sono, per esempio, quella del Levi, che, pur partendo dalla base degli schema *a minore* ed *a maggiore*, propone molteplici "soluzioni" ricavate dall' entità dei membri componenti l'unità del verso e riesce as ottenare per l'endecasillabo tre formule fondamentali e ben ottocentoventotto varietà di queste (19), e quella de Festa, che nell' endecasillabo trova un' analogia di struttura e d' articolazioni con un tipo di esametro e de trimetro tripartito in unità tirmiche minore o *kola* da lui segnalato e illustrato nella poesia greca (20):

> ed ecco/ verso noi/ venir per nave
> un vecchio/ bianco/ per antico pelo
> gridando./   Guai a voi, anime piave.   (Dante)—p. 17.

I am not suggesting the absence of Italian influence on Chaucer's prosody. I think the influence probably even greater than many scholars have suspected, but I think the influence stems from Dante's *De Vulgari Eloquentia* and not from Chaucer's attempts to capture the rhythms of the *endecasillabo*. No poet has ever satisfactorily appropriated for English poetry the identical rhythms of a foreign tongue. His rhythms must be native rhythms—the rhythms of good prose, and he must not depart too radically from the current prosodic rhythms if he hopes to be popular. Witness the situation that exists today. Some of our prominent literary historians are still unable to see anything but chaos in the rhythms of men like Eliot, Pound, Williams, and others. They have been unable to adjust their ears, accustomed to strongly iambic rhythm, to the freer rhythms of these poets. I shall, however, postpone discussion of Dante's probable influence until I have considered Chaucer's possible models.

The French Decasyllabic Myth

French has superseded Italian in popularity as a likely model for Chaucer's heroic line. But what are the facts ? Saintsbury

(*Hist. of Crit.*, II, 178) is wrong about the basis of French prosody. In French verse before the sixteenth century, he said, the iamb "had long been the only foot". This is sheer nonsense, because French verse is not, nor has it ever been iambic; and I think there is general agreement among French scholars on this matter. Let us approach the matter, however, from two points of view: the testimony of the prosodists and the evidence of those poets generally thought to exercise the greatest influence on Chaucer. Émile Faguet (*A Lit. Hist. of France*, 1907) explains the gradual loss of feeling for quantity, until by degrees the *number of syllables* became the basis, and points out that the medieval poets used the eight-syllable line, the ten-syllable, and later the twelve-syllable. He suggests that the ten-syllable line may be regarded, although this is more doubtful than his suggested source for the eight-syllable, as a departure from the Sapphic verse—

Abstulit clarum/ cita mors Achillem.

The last syllable was slurred, to render the line absolutely symmetrical, for it is noticeable that in the Middle Ages the decasyllabic line was *frequently broken up into two equal parts*. The twelve-syllable line only showed itself at a late epoch, near the end of the twelfth century (22, 23). Robert Bridges (*Milton's Prosody*, 1921), greatly dissatisfied with Skeat's treatment of Chaucer's prosody, not so much from the point of view of what Skeat wrote as from that of the way he read Chaucer and taught it, quotes M. Littré on the division of the twelve-syllable line into two hemistichs: "Autrefois l'hémistiche était considéré comme un fin de vers. Ainsi dans un poème du XIIIe siècle il est dit de Berthe:

Oncque plus douce chose ni vi, ne n'acointrai;
Elle est plus gracieuse que n'est la rose en mai."

This practice, says Bridges, invaded the ten-syllable verse, and, as this has no middle, it divided it unequally. He supports his statement in the following which contains two examples:

Quant vient en mai que l'on dit as lons jors,
Que Franc de France repairent de roi cort,
Reynauz repaire devant el premier front;
Si s'en passa lez lo meis Erembor,
Ainz n'en dengna la chief drecier amont.   (7)

Arthur Gosset (*op. cit.*) stresses the fact that "unlike English verse, French verse is not accentual" from which it follows that "French verse is properly measured not by *feet* or *beats*, but by syllables, and it must be possible to say of any French line with certainty, how many metrical syllables it contains". The idea of a prosody in feet or iambs is impossible. French verse, as I have pointed out in Chapter Two has only two dimensions, rhyme and metre; so that if one takes away the rhyme, it becomes invisible—in other words indistinguishable from prose. This explains, of course, the reason that, as I have already quoted, "les poëtes du moyen âge appelaient *vers* ce que nous appelons couplet," and that the single verse unit would be impossible.

M. Gosset points out that we should not confuse the French word *rhythme* with the sense in which we use the word rhythm. *Rhythme* and *rhythmique* are used to describe ingenious combinations of long and short words, alliteration, and so on. In a strict and technical sense, however, as when M. de Banville speaks of a poem as written "sur un beau rhythme emprunté à Ronsard," *rhythme* is merely the French for *meter* (7).

The following passages from Gosset, actually quotations from M. de Banville, bear directly on some of the misconceptions about Chaucer's prosody arising from the French influence:

"A French Verse is merely the union of a certain regular number of syllables, divided in some sorts of verse by a pause called a caesura, and always terminated by a sound *which only exists at the end of one verse on condition of being reproduced at the end of one or more other verses*, which repetition is called Rhyme" (10).

"When we speak of the number of metrical syllables in verses, we never count the final mute syllable of feminine rhymes" (27). In the body of the verse "every *e-* mute standing unsupported by a consonant and not forming the *last* syllable of a word, is suppressed altogether, and does not count as a syllable. This suppression is often represented in print by omitting the *e*, and putting the circumflex accent on the preceding vowel. Thus *flamboiement, avouerai,* count as three syllables each, flam-boî-ment, avoûrai; *louerais, nierons,* as two syllable each, loû-rais, nî-rons" (65).

"Till the fourteenth century the elision of vowels in a, i, o, u,

before an initial vowel or *h mute* was not contrary to the genius
of the French language" (76).   Quite possibly, Child appropriated
this earlier characteristic of French verse, and used it to explain
Chaucer's verse modelled on the Italian !   It is his contribution
to Tyrwhitt's theory !

Leon Clédat (*La Poésie lyrique et satirique en France au moyen
age*, Paris, n.d.) agrees with all the other writers on French
versification "sur le *nombre* des syllabes" (15).

When we turn from the prosodists to the poetry itself what
do we find ?   We need not concern ourselves with the influence
of Anglo-Norman French of the period because, as G. C. Macaulay
pointed out in his edition of Gower (I, xv), Anglo-Norman
literature had sunk to a very degraded condition, and such
authors as Pierre de Peccham, William of Waddington, Pierre
de Longtoft, and others, "had lost their hold on all the principles
of French verse and their metres [were] merely English in French
dress."   The verse of these writers consisted of two hemistichs
with "two accents each, irrespective of the number of unaccented
syllables, though naturally in English the irregularity is more
marked."   Or should we concern ourselves ?   No one would
suggest that Chaucer's verse is in "hemistichs of two accents
each", but it is one more possible rhythm that would be familiar
to the English audience.   This does not nullify, of course, the
influence of Anglo-Norman on spelling and pronunciation.

But what of the poetry of the French of Paris, the dialect
most probably affected by the most cultivated members of the
English court ?   The following individual lines from Deschamps
(quoted by Payne) certainly are not iambic:

> Saige ne foul, que Nature est formé
> Or est venu le très gracieux mai
> Angleterre, d'elle ce nom s'applique

But, as I have said, single lines are not enough.   The following
"Balade" (A Geffrey Chaucier) indicates that the rhetorical sense
permits of no iambic construction:

> Et de la rose, en la terre Angelique
> Qui d'Angela saxonne, et puis flourie
> Angleterre, d'elle ce nom s'applique
> Le derrenier en l'ethimologique.

Of the French writers, Guillaume de Machaut probably

exerted as great an influence on Chaucer's prosody as anyone. Chaucer's *rime-royal* stanza, for example, is that of many of the *balades* in *Le Livre De Voir-Dit* and *Poésies Lyriques*, among which we can cite "Véoir n'oïr ne puis riens que destourne," "Dès quon porroit les etoilles nombrer," "De mon vrai cuer jamais ne partira," "Gent corps, faitis, cointe, apert et joli," "Douce dame, que j'aim tant et desire," and others. Although it occasionally happens that the rhetorical pattern of a line of the foregoing, or of many of the *balades* in a different stanza pattern, falls into an iambic pattern, it is obvious that these *balades* support the theories of the prosodists that the accent is not fixed. The following, for example, is rather typical of the stanza movement:

> Pleurés, dames, pleurés vostre servant,
> Qui ay, tous dis, mis mon cuer & m'entente
> Corps & pensers & desirs, en servant
> L'onneur de vous que Dieus gart & augmente.

On the strength of the foregoing statements about French prosody and examples of French verse from the fourteenth century, how could Schipper assert that French employed a rising rhythm, or Ten Brink assert that the French iambic-decasyllabic was Chaucer's model when such a line did not exist? And how could Ten Brink apply to Chaucer the rules for elision (*caesure*) of *-e*, that were first formulated by Ronsard who with Du Bellay looked on French verse of the fourteenth century as crude as Dryden and Pope found the English poetry of the same period? Du Bellay (*La Defense et Illustration de la Langue Française*, Paris, 1930) thought of the poems of "those old French poets as groceries which corrupt the taste of our language and only serve to bear testimony to our ignorance" (85). Nor should we ignore Boileau's strictures against the poets of the *moyen âge*. He praised the contributions of the renaissance poets who brought order to French prosody in place of "le caprice tout seul" which earlier "faisait toutes les lois". It is important that he cited Villon as the first to effect a reform:

> Villon sut le premier, dans ces siècles grossiers,
> Debrouiller l'art confort de nos vieux romanciers.
>
>   —*Art Poetique*, Chant I

In the foregoing consideration of the influence of central French on Chaucer, we have further examples of the "Teutonic method" at work. If Chaucer used the iambic-decasyllable it must be apparent that it was not because he modelled his verse on French. I have already spoken of mute *e* in French and the rules for its treatment. Little need be said, therefore, of the many investigators who have thought Chaucer was influenced by its use.

Although I think the foregoing discussion rules out the possibility of the exclusive use of the Italian *endecasillabo* or the *non-existent* French iambic-decasyllable as Chaucer's model for his heroic line, we must entertain the idea that he may have worked from English models, modifying them to suit his need and borrowing ideas from the Italian and French which appealed to him. This, of course, is the method used by modern poets like Eliot, Pound, Auden, and others.

The Possibility of the English Tradition

We have many decasyllables, of course, in Old English. I read the following lines from *Beowulf* as such:

> Sigon þā to slǽpe. Sum sāre angeald
> ǽfenreste, swā him ful oft gelamp,
> Siþðan goldsele Grendel warode.
>
> 1251—1253

Professor Baum has pointed out the great variety of rhythms in *Beowulf* and has made a strong case for the possibility of a three-beat as against a two-beat verse.

The comparative regularity of contemporary verse—particularly the more learned verse—was mentioned by Bede (*Ars Metrica*): "Metrum est ratio cum modulatione: rhythmus modulatio sine ratione : plerumque tamen casu quodam invenies etiam rationem in rhythmus non artificis moderatione servatum, sed sono et ipsa modulatione ducente, quem vulgares poetae necesse est rustice, docti faciant docte". "*Rhythmus*," says Professor Baum, "as a name for vernacular verse sometimes ... describes a syllable-counting meter and sometimes a *modulatione sine ratione*, i.e. nonquantitative (*loc. cit.*, 75). Incidentally, Saintsbury's translation is misleading. Although of a much later date, Rolle's *Prick of Conscience* (c. 1350) and Robert of Gloucester's *Chronicle* (c. 1400) illustrate Bede's dictum.

Before examining any English verse, however, it is important to call attention to the scribes' use of the virgule (/). Many of

the best MSS of the fourteenth and fifteenth centuries employ
this mark within the lines. It is not a caesural mark in the way
in which we think of the caesura in classic or French verse, or,
for that matter, even in English verse. Some verses have none;
others have two; its position is not constant. It can occur
anywhere. Were it a true caesural mark it would of necessity
be placed within the foot and could or could not accord with
the pause in the sense. In many instances, were we reading
Chaucer's lines as iambic decasyllables, the virgule would fall
at the caesura. In the majority of cases, however, the virgule
falls at the end of the foot, or at the *diaeresis*. It is obvious
from Furnivall's remark about Hoccleve's use of the virgule—
a matter I shall discuss later—that the scholars of his period
did not understand it. Rightly understood, it is a valuable clue
to the person reading the verses aloud—the only one, since the
MSS carry no other mark of punctuation. "It is no part of the
pattern," to quote Mr. Lewis, "though it may be a very important part of the poet's handling of the pattern so as to move
passion or delight. It is a rhetorical and syntactical fact, not
a metrical fact" (29). The virgule is carefully used in the
Ellesmere, the Hengwrt, and others; sparingly used in Egerton
2726. Few of the Hoccleve MSS use it, although in HM 744
[Huntington MS] it is used carefully in the *Invocio ad patrem*,
but sparingly in *Lepistre de Cupide*. In HM 135 (Phillips MS
8980), in the *Regement of Princes*, the scribe uses no mark in
stanza 1, employs the · sparingly in stanza 2, both the · and
virgule in stanza 3, and from that point on the virgule almost
exclusively. The virgule is often so faint in the MSS that it
sometimes fails to show in the microfilm. The scribes of many
of the Lydgate MSS which I have examined were careful in its
use. In fact, the virgule does not disappear from MSS and
printed books until after Surrey, when there is no question that
a metrical system of prosody had succeeded a rhythmical
system. After Surrey, the decasyllabic line becomes increasingly
iambic, although in spite of what the critics decreed, the poets
continued to resist its too great dominance. It is not irrelevant
to remark that Surrey made his innovation when poetry was
being read silently rather than aloud and when the studies of
classical metres were being enthusiastically pursued. Furthermore in poems where the virgule is not regularly used, it fre-

quently occurs in passages where the rhythm would otherwise
be difficult. Interesting enough, too, is the fact that in the poems
in his own handwriting, Wyatt uses the virgule whenever the
rhythm might not be easily understood. Later, we shall examine
the poet's practice in greater detail. The foregoing is an
over-simplification and needs qualifying. Although the virgule
disappeared, the comma became the mark of a metrical rather
than a syntactical division. In *A Hundreth Sundrie Flowres*
(1573), for example, metrical punctuation occurs where syntactical requirements do not need it. The punctuation of lines 5, 12,
17, and 20 of "The careful lover combred with pleasure, thus
complayneth" appears to be metrical rather than logical:

And there to marke the jests, of every joyfull wight   (5)
Nor frame one warbling note to pass, out of hir
    mournfull voyce   (12)
But out alas my mind, amends not by their myrth   (17)
As mery medicines cannot serve, to kepe my corps
    from death   (20)

                              (*Quoted from Ing*, 83, 84)

The later collections of lyrics, according to Miss Ing (85), tended
to use metrical punctuation with less obviousness than did the
earlier collections. It should be readily apparent that we should
be far less dogmatic in this whole matter of prosody than the
late nineteenth-century scholars were.

    But to return to our examples. Rolle's verse, essentially
decasyllabic, can be tortured into an iambic pattern, but if it
is read so that the metrical pattern accords with the rhetorical
one, it is essentially rhythmical:

For seint Austyn seith þus in his holy boke

Let ever þin herte on the last ende loke

And whoso well þenkeþ in þis manere

And of all his synnes danseþ him heere

                                 —HM 128, f. 20r

The first part of Gloucester's *Chronicle* is a twelve-syllable verse divided into hemistichs.   In HM 126, the division is indicated by a · or by a virgule (/).   By the time we reach the later folio pages, however, the verse has become a predominantly ten-syllable one, although the hemistichs are still separated as before. In one instance, at least, we even have a nine-syllable line:

In þilk silf yer . as god yaf þat cas

—135 v. 27

The following have eleven syllables:

Of all Northumberlonde / among al þis wo

—73 r. 32

Seint Berm þe bishop / an holy man that was

—73 r. 37

"The goode wif thaught hir daughter . . ." (HM 128, f. 216v.) presents an interesting example of a popular form of rhythmical verse.   Written in irregular rhymed verses varying from ten to fourteen syllables, it is a rules-of-conduct poem:

O daughter ʒif you wilt ben a Wif / and wifeliche Werch

Look þt you love well god / and holy cherch

Go to cherch when þou myght / lette for no reyn

Al þe day þou fairest þe bette / þt þou hast god yseyn

The importance of this selection is that it indicates the basic rhythmic pattern of English verse at the time.   Chaucer's contribution was not to alter the basic rhythmical structure, but to regularize the line.   The well-known lyric "I sing of a myde that is makeles" (MS Sloane 2593) does not appear in the

MS as it appears in modern texts. The · is placed after *myde*, *kyngs*, *stylle*, and so forth. The lyric "Erthe upon erthe" (Coxe, *Catalogi Codicum, etc.*, Oxford, 1858 [MS Laud Misc. 23] further illustrates the type of line contemporary with Chaucer:

> When lyf is most lovyd ʒ' deeth is most hatyd:
> thanne deeth draweth his draut and makyth man ful nakid
> Erthe out of erthe is wõdirly wrouʒt
> Erthe upon erthe · hath get a dignyte of nowth
> Erthe upon erthe · hath set al his thouʒt
> How that erthe up on erthe may be hyʒ browth
> Erthe up on erthe wolde be a kyng; but
> how erthe shal to erthe thinkiþ he no thig /
> Whã that erthe biddeth erthe his rentys
> hoom bring: thanne shal erthe out of the
> erthe have a peto [?] partyng /
> Erthe upon erthe wynneth cattellis and touris / thane
> [?] ferth erthe to erthe . this is al ouris.

It would be a simple matter to multiply the examples. The investigator should not, of course, neglect the basic similarity in the rhythms of Chaucer and *Piers Plowman*. But one thing is obvious. Neither from the Italian, French, or English could Chaucer borrow the iambic decasyllabic line, nor one in which there is the regular alternation of unstressed and stressed syllables. Nor would Medieval Latin be of much help, because its rhythms are trochaic or rhythmical. What, then, did he do ?

Of one thing we can be certain. If Chaucer's prosody had differed as markedly from the English tradition as later nineteenth-century scholars seemed to think, he would not have been immediately popular. The greater the alteration of the poetic tradition of any country the slower will be the acceptance of the poetry causing the alteration. It has taken Mr. T. S. Eliot thirty years to reach his present acceptance, and he is still caviar to the general. After the certain introduction of the iambic-decasyllable by Surrey, much poetry still maintained a rhythmical character. It would be difficult, indeed, to scan much of the dialogue of Shakespeare's plays as basically iambic, although many set passages are often quite regular. The closed couplet presents another interesting analogy. Although used by Ben Johson, and more extensively by Waller, it did not become the predominant form until Pope and the eighteenth century. If Chaucer were introducing the iambic decasyllable we should expect to find considerable resistance to his innovation and a delayed popularity; but we find none. Furthermore, we should expect his avowed disciples to imitate him.

It is now fitting that we consider the possible influence of Dante's *De Vulgari Eloquentia* on Chaucer. If a poet were to write in the vernacular, Dante believed that he should investigate the several poetic forms *available* to him, select the one that best accords with the qualities he seeks, and then find the verse pattern that is most effective for the poetic form he has chosen. To deal with exalted subjects, he believed the poet's vocabulary must be *illustrious, cardinal, courtly,* and *curial.* He chose the *canzone* as the noblest and most worthy, and the *endecasillabo* as the stateliest. How did Chaucer find the answers to these dicta ?

Chaucer's vocabulary contains a much greater percentage of French words than that of any of his predecessors, but this is easily explained. His social and economic position accounts for it. According to Professor Baugh (*History of the English Language,* 207) "the upper classes carried over into English an astonishing number of common French words. In changing from French to English they transferred much of their governmental and administrative vocabulary, their ecclesiastical, legal, and military terms, their familiar words of fashion, food, and social life, the vocabulary of art, learning, and medicine." These borrowings include the words which Dante believed were necessary to fulfil his four conditions. Chaucer chose English in preference to French and the decasyllabic verse to the octosyllabic verse which Machaut in *Le Livre Du Voir-Dit* and Deschamps in *Le Miroir de Mariage* had used in the narrative parts of their poems. He did this instead of doing as did his friend Gower who wrote in all three languages known by an educated person. English prose was already a highly deleveloped instrument. It is possible that in choosing a verse that is essentially decasyllabic instead of an octosyllabic one he realized from his own earlier practice, as did Byron from his, the difficulty of triumphing "over the fatal facility of the octosyllabic verse". The heroic line in English was often predominantly

decasyllabic; that of the French regularly so. His great contribution was the regularization of the essentially decasyllabic
line already frequently used in English, and the more complete
naturalization of French words which would elevate English
to the position of dignity where it would satisfy Dante's requirements. In other words, he merely used the vocabulary with
which he was thoroughly familiar. The conscious influence of
Dante is, of course, pure supposition, although Chaucer made
his choice after his first visit to Italy. It is apparent, however,
from his many statements about the writer's craft that no poet
was more conscious of his aesthetic problem than he.

Let us briefly review the materials that were available to him.
The *endecasillabo* so suitable to the Italian language with its
great possibilities for feminine rhymes was not suitable to
English with its preponderance of masculine rhymes.   The
structure of the line itself, however, was as Signor Levi has
pointed out, essentially rhythmical in that 828 variations of the
line were possible through the various combinations of settenario
+ quinario, quinario + settenario, and quinario + senario.
It does not lend itself to analysis by classical feet. In the light
of Signor Levi's analysis of the types, does not this make Child's
unsupported statement that Tyrwhitt was right in Chaucer's
use of the *endecasillabo* as his model a presumptuous one ?

In French, Chaucer had a line regular in length, divided about
the middle by a long pause, and rhythmical in nature.   There
are no feet in French verse, the mute *e* is not sounded in speaking,
except very slightly in conjunction with certain consonants, any
stress that does occur is rhetorical, and the *vers* was what we
should call a couplet.

In English, he had a line divided into hemistichs, the number
of syllables varied greatly in popular poetry but was fairly
regular in more learned or more elevated poetry, frequently being
essentially decasyllabic. It was rhythmical in nature and was
not thought of in foot-units. The break between Old English,
early and late Middle English is not so great as it has been
thought to be—prosodically speaking, at least.

Chaucer's problem, therefore, was to preserve the essential
basic English rhythm, increase the poetic vocabulary, regularize
the line, and yet give it the fluidity possessed by French and
Italian. We might even say that his task was to capture in

verse the highly developed, colloquial, energetic speech of the cultivated classes with whom he was in intimate contact. But of one thing we can be certain, his line could not be the iambic pentameter because the appreciation of this verse is not a simple matter. Whether it be the iambic pentameter of Dryden, Pope, or Mr. Frost, the poet superimposes on the basic pattern the rhythms of colloquial speech. The reader, therefore, must possess what Mr. Lewis calls "double audition". This, Mr. Lewis says, "must be the growth of long training and for which nothing in their previous experience had prepared the Englishman of Chaucer's time. If this is so, two questions arise: 1. Is it probable that Chaucer himself had caught the music of the modern decasyllable and intended his countrymen to hear this music in his own verse ? 2. Even if Chaucer did so intend, is it at all possible that they would have understood him ?" (31). We have already examined some of the London prose of Chaucer's day and the rhythms in the letters of Lady Zouche, and have seen, as is also evident in Chaucer's own prose, that the final unaccented *-e* was probably not pronounced. The matter of his pronunciation in his poetry is still an open matter, and we must defer our opinion until we have the evidence of the MSS themselves.

It is unfortunate that we have no contemporary evidence about fourteenth-century verse. Chaucer makes one reference to it in the *Hous of Fame*—

> To make bookys, songes, dytees,
> In rime, or elles in cadence   —622, 623

Lydgate also speaks of Chaucer's "verses of cadence", but does not define cadence. Could we gloss "or elles" as "otherwise" ? Undoubtedly the term was understood and accepted by his contemporaries and followers, or someone would have defined it, especially had it differed markedly from the tradition in which those who recognized him as their master were working. Gascoigne has given us the first description of Chaucer's verse. Although he probably erred in thinking of Chaucer's verse as four-stressed, it does give a good idea of its rhythmical character and of Gascoigne's regret at the gradual domination of the iamb:

> "Also our father Chaucer hath used the same libertie in
> feete and measures that the Latinists do use: and who so

ever do peruse and well consider his workes, he shall finde
that although his lines are not always of one selfe same
number of syllables, yet, beying redde by one that hath
understanding, the longest verse, and that which hath the
most Syllables in it, will fall (to the eare) correspondent unto
that which hath the fewest sillables in it; and likewise that
whiche hath in it fewest syllables shalbe founde yet to consist of woordes that have suche naturall sounde, as may
seeme equall in length to a verse which hath many more
sillables of lighter accentes.   And surely I can lament that
wee are fallen into such a playne and simple manner of
wryting, that there is none other foote used but one;
wherby our Poemes may iustly be call Rithmes, and cannot
by any right challenge the name of a Verse.   But, since it
is so, let us take the forde as we finde it, and lette me set
downe unto you suche rules or precepts that even in this
playne foot of two syllables you wrest no woorde from his
natural and usuall sounde."

It is obvious from Gascoigne's statement that a musical
notation is the only one that adequately can capture Chaucer's
music. I think, too, that by the end of our investigation we shall
understand what Chaucer meant by "cadence", and that the idea
of foot was unknown to him.

To this point, then, our investigation has led us.   We must
begin afresh on the basis of the MSS themselves; and this was
the point to which Manly had come by the time he finished his
edition of the *Canterbury Tales*: "It is still uncertain," he wrote,
"whether Chaucer's versification should always have the regularity assumed for it by scholars of the late 19 C.   Certainly
lines of trochaic movement, lacking the unstressed syllable of
the first foot, are far more numerous in the MSS than any earlier
editor has admitted.   Current theories of Chaucer's versification
are based, not upon the text as found in the MSS, or as established
by critical processes, but upon an artificial text made regular
by all the devices at the disposal of the scholar."   (*CT*, II, 40,
41).

What then is the evidence afforded by the MSS ?   We must
be careful I think, in speaking of any regular number of stresses;
and modern prosodists are chary of such terminology.   As
Professor Van Doren has pointed out so clearly in the analyses

in his *Introduction to Poetry*, the only real stresses in a line are the rhetorical stresses. It is easily possible to manipulate the reading of Chaucer's verses so that there are five rhetorical stresses in the line. Often, however, the stresses vary from four to six or seven. In the matter of scanning poetry dogmatism has no place. This earlier freedom, once again established, was not permitted by the end of the seventeenth century, although greater freedom was permitted than is generally believed. Dryden ("An Essay of Dramatic Poesy," in Ker, I, 97) said: "No man is tied in modern poesy to observe any further rule in the feet of his verse, but that they be dissyllables; whether spondee, trochee, or iambic, it matters not." Today we have returned to the freedom possible to Chaucer.

CHAPTER FOUR

THE TESTIMONY OF THE MANUSCRIPTS: CHAUCER

IN the preceding chapter, I attempted to clear away the matter that has obscured the facts of Chaucer's prosody. It is important that we abandon the practice of "establishing out of thin air a hypothetical *typus* without regard to facts." But to what materials can we go for our facts ? Unfortunately, no published text can give us all that we need, and we must have recourse to the MSS themselves. Even the admirable Manly-Rickert text is unsuitable, because the editors made no attempt to list all deviations in the use of final unaccented *-e*, and they did not follow the practice of the best MSS in the use of the virgule. This is a rhetorical mark, and of great use to the prosodist.

It will be readily apparent, however, that the theory I shall advance will fit the Manly-Rickert text, just as it will fit every one of the MSS, regardless of divergences in spelling. In many instances it will not fit the Skeat text because of Skeat's unwarranted emendations. It will fit the Robinson text better, but will still be unsatisfactory. The theory will also fit the Globe text if the reader ignores the editors' indication of a silent or sounded final *-e*. We must ignore many of the early texts of the Chaucer and Early English Text Society because the editors were, according to Professor Zupitza (*Phil. Soc. Trans.*, 1877-79, p. 11., quoted by Henry Sweet), "dilettantes" with "very vague ideas of philological method, of the treatment of the text, especially when it is preserved in several MSS," with much more in a derogatory vein. In other words, in testing the theory we must be certain that the texts are reliable.

Valuable as the Manly-Rickert text is as an archetype, Sir William Craigie believed, and often told Manly so, that the interests of the scholar could most effectively be served by printing two or three of the best MSS of Chaucer rather than by attempting to establish the archetype.[7] Printing several versions of the same lyric was, of course, the method used by Carleton Brown in his three valuable volumes of medieval lyrics.

I have chosen the MSS which, except for Additional 5140, the paleographers agree were nearest in date to Chaucer, and so should most nearly represent his pronunciation. Before examining the MSS, however, some word should be said about the scribes, because no one thinks that the MSS represent Chaucer's own spelling. At least no one does today, although some of the earlier investigators—notably the Germans—apparently thought so. The MSS were written by scribes in lay workshops, but there is no evidence of complete uniformity of spelling by even the scribes in the same shop. The scribes in the workshops, however, were probably of the scrivener class. As such they could be depended upon to have some understanding of the work being copied and of the prosodic form. The following MSS form the basis of my discussion: Merthyr, c. 1400; Hengwrt (Hg), 1400—1410; Ellesmere (El), 1400—1410; Harley 7334, c. 1410; with additional illustrations from Additional 10340, c. 1400; and Additional 5140, 1470—1500.

The Merthyr, which is but a fragment of the "Nun's Priest's Tale," is in "one good book hand, of the same general type as El Hg" (Manly-Rickert, I, 361). "The dialect is East Midland; the only forms that seem out of the ordinary are: keen = kine, height = highte, flaugh = flew, hundreth. The loss of many final *e*'s—note especially the definite adjective—and the presence of some scribal *e*'s suggest that the language is rather modern for 1400" (*Ibid.*, I, 362).

The Hengwrt, probably written by the same scribe as the Ellesmere, "is remarkably close to the Ellesmere in dialect forms and in spelling" although it "is somewhat less regular" (*Ibid.*, I, 276). The placement of the virgule or "punctuation . . . is about the same in kinds and quantity as in El, but there are enough differences in the position of the caesural strokes in the lines of verse to suggest that they were not copied from the same exemplar but put in by the scribes independently" (*Ibid.*, I, 278). Notice that Manly is not wholly consistent. In one instance he speaks of the single scribe for both the El and the Hg; in another he speaks of the scribes. But is he correct in his assumption that the scribes were responsible for the position of the virgules or prosodial bars ? We cannot know positively, but in the light of what we shall discover when we examine the MSS of Wyatt's poems—that it is only in those in his own handwriting that the virgule appears, and then only to clarify difficult rhythmical passages—it is not impossible that the scribe(s) of the El and Hg were working from different versions of Chaucer's own holograph.[8]   Because, however, of its "great freedom from accidental errors and its entire freedom from editorial variants," Manly considered the Hg "of the highest importance" (*Ibid.*, I, 276).

The Ellesmere, a carefully supervised MS, although long "regarded by many scholars as the single MS of most authority, its total of unique variants, many of which are demonstrable errors, is approximately twice that of Hg, as is also the total of slips shared with the other MSS by *acco*. . . . The MS may well have been made in London. . . . Slight indications of Northern influence may be only those that might appear in London English. While there are some lapses, the final *e* is treated with unusual care" (*Ibid.*, I, 150, 151).   To a certain degree Manly would seem to contradict himself, however, when he says that the virgule "is placed with evident care, usually as in Hg" (152).

The Harley 7334 is in "one excellent book hand . . . similar to the hand in Egerton 1991," and "the dialect features are similar to those of Cp [Corpus Christi, 1410—1420] (*Ibid.*, I, 220, 222).   Additional 10340 is useless from the point of view of establishing a text because it was "apparently written from memory, with omissions and transpositions of lines" (*Ibid.*, I, 48, 49).   From the prosodist's point of view it can be of value, because I think most readers will agree that when quoting from memory we may garble the text, but we do keep the verse pattern reasonably correct.

I think scholars agree that such popular fourteenth century works as the *Gest Hystoriale of the Destruction of Troy, Piers Plowman, Sir Gawayne and the Grene Knyght* are rhythmical and not metrical, and most, at least, also agree that final *e* in these works was not pronounced.   Although the verses belong generally to the hemistich tradition, the division of the lines into two parts is much freer than is customary in the poetry of an earlier century.   It has been customary to think of these works as belonging to a tradition different from that of the poetry of Chaucer, possibly because of the prominence of alliteration. Chaucer, it is true, disliked the excessive *rim, ram, ruff* of these poets, but it would not be safe to assume that because he uses alliteration more sparingly than they, the basic rhythm of his verses would markedly differ.   As Miss Dorothy Everett has pointed out ("Chaucer's 'Good Ear'", *RES*, XXXII (July, 1947), 201—208), Chaucer not only has such lines as "Flemere of feendes out of hym and here," but often makes extensive use of alliteration in some of his most striking scenes. Such innovations as he wished to make must be made within limits. If his rhythms differed too radically, he could not have been, as Mr. C. S. Lewis has pointed out, immediately popular. Chaucer's stresses must, therefore, also have been rhetorical rather than metrical. Even, however, if Chaucer had ignored the English tradition in favour of the French, as most American scholars seem to believe (and I think erroneously), his stresses must still have been rhetorical. Unfortunately, French prosody was misunderstood by many Chaucerian scholars of the nineteenth century, notably Schipper and Ten Brink. Obviously many verses read rhetorically will fall into an iambic pattern, just as sentences in prose often fall into such a pattern. But to think that this is the norm is the root of the evil.

If the reader pronounces Chaucer's final *e*'s many more lines will be iambic than otherwise; but he will also find that if he is consistent many lines will be "broken-backed". For example, the first complete line of the Merthyr fragment, NP 3998, can be read as strictly iambic if we pronounce the *e* in *rude*, or rhetorically if the *e* is silent as it probably was in speech and prose:

(rhetorical) | ♪. | ♩ ♪ | ♩ ♪ | ♩. | ♩ ♪ | ♩.
(iambic) ♪ | ♩ ♪ | ♩ ♪ | ♩♪ | ♩ ♪ | ♩ (♪)
Than spake oure hoost with rude speche and bolde

In the conventional notation, I think the scansion could be indicated as follows:

(rhythmical) / / | ⌣ / | ⌣ / | / ⌣ | /
(iambic) ⌣ / | ⌣ / | ⌣ / | ⌣ / | ⌣ / (⌣)

To me the variations in the first line give a beauty that the regularity of the second does not give. And, of course, the variations of the first are so numerous that to list them all would be a laborious and useless task. The subtle nuances of time are lost by such a notation for either line.

In line 4,000, only one reading is possible—

| ♩. | ♩. | ♩ ♪ | ♩ ♪ | ♩ ♪ | ♩.
telle s[wi]ch thyng as may our hertes glade—

unless, of course, the reader insists on the final *e* (♪), in which case the notation would be | ♩ ♪ .

In 4,001, *blyth* has no final *e*

| ♪. | ♩. | ♩   ♪ | ♩ ♪| ♩♪| ♩.

Be blyth though thow ride upon a jade

And 4,002, *both* is also without final *e*

| ♪. | ♩   ♪ | ♩⌐| ♩ ♪ | ♩ ♪ | ♩

What though [thyn] hors be both foule and [lene]

It is obvious that the following examples can be read in two ways, one with a metrical accent, the other with a rhetorical accent. Since there is little evidence in the poetry of Chaucer's contemporaries, or, as I hope to show in that of his disciples, for a metrical accent, I think it unlikely that Chaucer employed what did not exist in English, French, or Italian at the time he wrote or before. Quite obviously practices that came in with Ronsard, Du Bellay, and others have no bearing on the case, although several nineteenth-century scholars wrote as if they did.

(rhythmical) ♪ ♪. ♪.| ♩ |♪.|♪. | ♪ ♩| ♪. ♪.
(iambic) ♪| ♩ ♪| ♩ ♪| ♩ ♪| ♩ ♪| ♩

And in this cart he lith gapyng upryght

(rhythmical) | ♪. | ♩ ♪ | ♩.|♪.♪.| ♩.| ♩. | ♩.
(iambic) ♪ | ♩ ♪| ♩ ♪| ♩ ♪| ♩♪| ♩

What sholde I more unto this tale sayne

(rhythmical) ♪| ♩. | ♩. | ♩♪| ♩. ♪.| ♩
(iambic) ♪| ♩♪| ♩♪| ♩♪| ♩ ♪ | ♩

On Masse dayes þat in cherches goon

Granted the difference is slight, but there is a difference. I have remarked that English poetry was essentially in 3/8 time. It is questionable, however, whether a poet as subtle as Chaucer does not often use a combination of 3/8 and 2/8 time, a combination used by Tennyson, that great master of verbal music.

The effect of the use of the virgule will be considered in our illustrations from the Hengwrt and Ellesmere MSS, and in even greater detail when we examine the prosody of Hoccleve, the one poet we know who may have been acquainted with Chaucer and even worked under him. But what of those lines in the Merthyr fragment that do not scan as iambic ? Must we assume that a good scribe omitted letters necessary to the scansion, or are we to suspect the scansion that has supplanted the one *traditional until* Child ? Unless we know facts about the scansion from other sources—which we do not know—I prefer suspecting the scansion, especially if it is in keeping with practices of other poets.

Wel sikerer was his crowyng in his logge / Than is a clock

4043,4

Oof the quynoxial in thilk toun

4046

That ye had h'rd the ded man devyse

4228

The ded man t[ha]t morthered was al new

4239

Mordure is so wlatsom and so abhomynable

4243

That god þᵗ is so iuste and so resonable

4244

Mordre wil oute this is my conclusion

4247

The chief effect of dropping the final *e* is the longer time received by the root vowel, especially the long vowels that are really long. This is, according to Professor Kökeritz (*A Guide*, etc., p. 3, rule 1) as they should be. Many of the words in the Merthyr, as Manly has pointed out have no final *e*. We have, as I have said, *keen, height, blyth, hert, thilk, ded, said, brought, never, sklender, blys, couth, trew, gret*:

Three keen and eke a sheep þᵗ height malle   4021
In which she ete ful many a sklender mele   4023

Madame Patelote my worldes blys   4389
And if a rethor couth [fa]ire endi[te]   4396
T[hat] women hold in gret rever[ence]   4402
That thilk day was p[erilous] to thee   4422

Let us turn now to the Hengwrt MS for such evidence as we may find.   First, let us examine the scribe's use of the virgule. Unfortunately the first folio of the MS is badly smudged, but from what I can make out, the virgule appears only once, in line 7 after *croppes*.   From the fourth line of f. 2, however, the scribe employs it.   It appears in the following positions in the Hengwrt:

after the second syllable:

And heeld / after the newe world the space   176
Therefore / he was a prykasour aright   189
And wende / for to doon his pilgrymage   78

after the third syllable:

A lovere / and a lusty bachiler   80
At that tyme / for him liste ryde so   102
And after / amor vincit omnia   162

after the fourth:

Of his stature / he was of evene lengthe   83
He was as fresh / as is the monthe of may   92
And by his syde / a swerd and a bokeler   112

after the fifth:

Al bismotered / with his haubergeon   76
A yeman he hadde / and servauntz namo   101
A not heed hadde he / with a broun visage   109

after the sixth:

Wel koude he sitte on hors / and faire ryde   94
Curteys he was, lowely / and servysable   99
That was hir chapelayne / and preestes three   164

after the seventh:

Short was his goune with sleves / longe and wyde   93
And carf biforn his fader / at the table   100
A sheef of pecock arwes / bright and keene   104

dual virgule

In fflaundres / in Artoys / and Picardye   86
On which / was first writen / a crowned. A.   161
He hadde / of gold / wroght a ful curious pyn   196
A fat swan / loved he / best of any roost   206

In 100 lines (80—179) we have the following distribution:

  5 after the second syllable (79, 127, 135, 176, 178)

  8 after the third syllable (80, 86, 102, 110, 131, 162, 175, 180)

  33 after the fourth syllable (81, 83, 87, 91, 92, 96, 103, 108, 111, 112, 118, 120, 124, 125, 134, 136, 137, 145, 147, 148, 151, 152, 153, 154, 156, 158, 163, 165, 166, 167, 169, 171, 172)

  14 after the fifth syllable (88, 89, 101, 109, 117, 121, 126, 128, 129, 141, 142, 149, 159, 173)

  12 after the sixth syllable (85, 90, 95, 99, 113, 123, 143, 150, 157, 164, 168, 174)

  6 after the seventh syllable (84, 94, 100, 104, 130, 170)

  3 with two virgules (115 (4, 6), 146 (4, 6), 161 (2, 6))

  18 with no virgule (82, 97, 98, 105, 106, 107, 115, 116, 119, 122, 132, 138, 139, 140, 155, 160, 177)

Two lines have no virgule but employ a = (133), or a · (179).

In the "Miller's Tale", the distribution (Ellesmere) is as follows: after the second syllable, 10; after the third, 7; after the fourth, 43; after the fifth, 14; after the sixth, 8; after the seventh, 1; after the eighth, 2; dual virgule, 6; and no virgule, 11. In the "Nun's Tale", we have after the second, 5; after the third, 8; after the fourth, 44; after the fifth, 13; after the sixth, 12; after the seventh, 3; after the eighth, 1; dual virgule, 3; none, 11. It had occurred to me before I began my actual count that the distribution would be less regular in those tales of a more colloquial nature, and to a slight extent the count of the "Miller's Tale" might indicate this, but I do not think the evidence conclusive from 99, 102, and 100 lines respectively.

Of the 40 lines that have no virgule, every one has a caesura as it is understood by the proponents of the iambic theory, although it was not, as I pointed out in Chapter Three, strictly a caesura in the classical sense. A careful examination would also reveal, I think, that in those lines where the virgule is used, it does not always appear at the caesural pause. It is, therefore, a rhetorical and not a metrical mark. At a time when popular poetry was so extensively divided into more or less equal hemistichs, the virgule is in some measure a guide to the reader. We shall see when we examine the prosody of Hoccleve, Lydgate, Wyatt, and others, that Hoccleve understood the subtlety of Chaucer's rhythms and tried to capture them. Lydgate lacked

Chaucer's subtle ear and his verses degenerate into a smooth pattern in the same way that much of the poetry in iambic decasyllabic couplets in the nineteenth century degenerated from the beautiful modulations that we find in those of Dryden and Pope.

My own experience is that by paying strict attention to the virgule, I find that Chaucer's verse takes on the qualities of conversational prose of the type listed in the previous chapter. This was particularly true when I no longer pronounced the final *e*'s. In only two lines did I find in any way awkward the rhetorical reading without sounding the final *e* :

> At that tyme / for hym lyste ryde so
> Ne wette hir fyngres / in hir sauce deepe

Was the *e* of *liste* and of *sauce* sounded ? The Hengwrt gives us no clue, but Harley 7334 does for *liste*, because it reads "At þat tyme for him lust ryde soo." Actually, neither *e* is necessary

♪ ♪ | ♩· | ♩· | ♩·
for hym lyste ride so

♪ ♪ | ♩· | ♩·
in hir sauce deepe

The root vowel of *liste* and *sauce* is merely given the full time, instead of | ♩ ♪. The *e* of *sauce* would not be sounded in A. Prol. 351, B. NP 4024, C. Pard. 545, Form. A. 16. Incidentally, the scribe of Hengwrt treats one passage in a way that leads me to believe that modern editors have mispunctuated the passage. The MS reading is as follows:

> Hir ouer lyppe = wyped she so cleene
> That in hir coppe / ther was no ferthing seene
> Of grece / Whan she dronken hadde hir draughte
> fful semely / after hir mete she raghte.

The capital W is obvious, and a period should follow *grece*. *Fful semely* modifies *dronken* and not *raghte*. A slight hesitation at the virgule is similar to the pause that a story-teller would make to give the sense of spontaneity to his narration.

Let me attempt to present the description of the prioress with a musical notation as well as with the conventional metrical notation, remembering always that different readers will sometimes place the stresses differently. Every person, not a

Chaucerian scholar, to whom I have read Chaucer has preferred
the rhetorical to the metrical reading. The person familiar with
the usual reading must accustom his ear to the rhythmical.
At first it is almost bound to seem strange; perhaps as strange
as was sounding the *e's* to the 19 C scholars when Child wrote
his "Observations". His statement was whether or not the
reader liked it, it was so. I should prefer to be less dogmatic;
but the ear must adjust itself.

Ther was also / a nonne a pri o resse   118

That of hir smy ling was ful sym ple and coy   119

Hir gretteste ooth / was but by Seint Loy   120

And she was cle pyd / ma dame Eg lan tine   121

fful wel she soong the ser vyce dy vyne   122

Entuned in hir nose / ful semely   123

And frenssh she spak / ful faire and fe tis ly   124

Af ter the scole / of S[trat for]d at the Bowe   125

ffor frenssh of Paris / was to hire un knowe   126

At mete / wel y taught was she with alle   127

She leet no morsel / from hir lip pes falle   128

Ne wette hir fyn gres / in hir sauce deepe   129

Wel koude she carve a mor sel / and wel keepe   130

That no drop / fille up on hir brest   131

In curtesye was set mu chel hir list   132

I think line 125 with *at the* (Hg) instead of *atte* as we find it in most editions, indicates a different stress than is usually accorded the line. It would be | ♩♪ | ♩, rather than | ♪♪ | ♪♪.

From the point of view of traditional notation, what do we have ? Line 131 has eight syllables, lines 120, 122, 127, and 129 have nine each, line 119, eleven, and the rest ten. It is difficult, if not impossible, to think of all the lines as comprising five feet. Lines 121 and 126 are the only ones in which the unstressed and stressed syllables alternate regularly, but these are not strictly iambic, because, as I have pointed out, in a regular iamb the unstressed element of the foot receives only half the time of the stressed element. And if we heed the virgule, the second element of each verse is essentially trochaic. Except for these two lines, no others scan in exactly the same manner. We have spondees, trochees, pyrrhics, amphibrachs, and dactyls in various combinations, and too frequently to permit our calling the verse iambic pentameter. Rhetorical or rhythmical are the only terms general enough to cover the facts, unless, of course, we use Chaucer's term. Quite possibly, when he spoke of his "verses of cadence" it was to these verses that he was referring. In other words, to speak of his verses as "rhythmical" implies that Chaucer's interest was the same as that of all good poets—an interest in the internal structure of the line. He realized, I think, that the great use of alliteration, so characteristic of the poetry of his predecessors and contemporaries, tended to minimize the interest in the more important matters of rhythm. The same is true of too great an interest in rhyme. The great weakness of much of the late nineteenth century American

97899

poetry is the attention to the end of the line rather than to its inner structure.   Ezra Pound's great contribution, of course, is that he recalled the attention of poets to the most important aspect of their craft.

What evidence do we find in other MSS to support our contentions ?   Line 74 of Hengwrt reads "His hors weere goode but he ne was nat gay."   Was the -e of goode pronounced ? In Harley 7334 this line reads "His hors was good but he ne was nat gay."   The rhetorical stress is the same for each, but read as iambic lines the change to the singular preserves the regular metre.   Line 84 of Hengwrt reads "And wonderly delyvere / and of gr[ete str]engthe."   Read as an iambic line the -e of grete would be sounded.   There is a change in word order in Harley 7334, and the last half of the line reads "and gret of strengthe" with no -e on gret.   Read rhetorically the stresses fall in the same way:

$$\times \quad / \quad \smile \quad /$$
and gret of strengthe
$$\times \quad \smile \quad / \quad \quad /$$
and of gret strengthe

Line 121 in Hengwrt reads "clepyd", but in Harley 7334 we have "clept" before the virgule.   Whether it is a dissyllable or a monosyllable the rhythm is not disturbed when read rhetorically, because the first syllable of Madame received the stress in either case.

Let us take a familiar example, the opening of the Prologue. The following is from the Ellesmere:

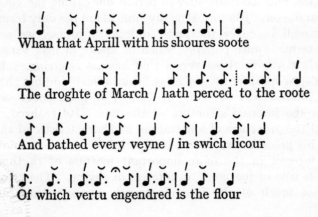

Whan that Aprill with his shoures soote

The droghte of March / hath perced to the roote

And bathed every veyne / in swich licour

Of which vertu engendred is the flour

Whan zephirus eek with his swetee breeth

Inspired hath / in every holt and heeth

The tendre croppes / and the yonge sonne

Hath in the ram / his half cours yronne

And smale foweles / maken melodye

That slepen al the nyght / with open eye

So priketh hem nature in hir corages

Thanne longen folk / to goon on pilgrimages

And palmeres / for to seken straunge strondes

To ferne halwes / kowthe in sondry londes

And specially fram every shires ende

Of Engelond / to Caunterbury they wende

The holy blisful martir for to seke

That hem hath holpen whan that they were seeke

The passage could be read much more subtly than I have indicated, often with four or six stresses rather than five. An analysis of the stresses indicates that this passage has more iambs than the passage from the description of the prioress. The readings which are most open to question by those sceptical of the thesis I am attempting to develop are probably *straunge* and *ferne* treated as monosyllabic rather than as dissyllabic, and "his half cours yronne". The last is most easily disposed of because as Manly has pointed out *half cours* is the reading of the best MSS. Additional 5140 helps us out with *ferne* because the spelling there is without the *e*. The usual explanation would be to ascribe its omission to a scribal error. Had it been pronounced would the error be so likely as if it were silent ?

Does Chaucer's prose help us in any way ? As an adverb *fern* appears once in the *Squire's Tale* (256). As an adjective, it appears once in the prose with the *e*, but the rhythm would indicate that it was probably not sounded—"For although that renoun ysprad, passynge to ferne peples, goth by diverse tonges" (Robinson, 398, 11a—13a). What is the treatment of the *e* of *straunge* in the prose ? We have

to the eyres of straunge folk	Bo. 2. p. 4, 386-90
Why embracest thow straunge goodes	Bo. 2. p. 5, 435-40
how schal straunge or foreyne goodnesse	
	Bo. 2. p. 5, 445-50
peraventure among straunge nacions	Bo. 3. p. 4, 705-10
you fro alle straunge folk, and fro lyeres	
	B. Mel. 2495-500

As I earlier pointed out, the idea that Chaucer's pronunciation in his prose differs from that in his verse is essentially a myth founded on a misunderstanding. And if his pronunciation of his verse did differ from that of his prose then he is unique in the world of poets. The nineteenth-century poets did indulge in poetic licence at times, and Goethe with whom Chaucer has been compared was one. But I have already pointed out the weakness of attempting to explain Chaucer's practice by an analogy with Goethe's practice. But to return to our passage. We find *good* without an *e* (RR 3943), *close* spelt *cloos*, *grete* spelt *gret* (*gret penaunce* TC, 1. 94, *gret love* Bo. 5. m. 3. 1725-30), *yerde* spelt *yerd* and *yeerd*, *thilke*, also spelt *thilk*, *ilke* and *ilk* and so on. It was pronounced without the *e* (*ilk*) in Hoccleve.   The *e* of *aven-ture* is not only silent before *h* or a vowel, but also before *this* (AKn 1516) and *was* (AKn 2703) even if read as an iambic line.

But what of the slight alterations in many lines that destroy the iambic pattern ?   In the description of the Prioress Hengwrt has a virgule after *grece* which is spelt *grees* in Harley 7334, a spelling which destroys the iambic pattern.   So, too, does the insertion of *I* before *pynched* (151), and the insertion of *þat* before *Amor* (162).   Oxf. Bodl. Laud. misc. 600 contains as many deviations as Harley 7334, but not one of the deviations destroys the rhythmical pattern.

I have mentioned that Additional 10340 was valueless for textual purposes, because, apparently written from memory, there are interchanges and omissions of lines.   Out of the 32 lines at least six cannot be read as iambic decasyllables, but they all read well rhythmically:

> and was a goode man of religeoune
> holy he was both in þouȝt and werk
> Was his parrish housed naught so far a sondir
> þis noble ensample un to his shepe he ȝaf
> þo ran to London unto saynt poules
> oþer wiþ a breþerhed to be wiþholde

We have tauȝt and rauȝt, myskarry and mercenary without final *-e*; and *hold* without final *-e* rhyming with *wiþholde* with final *e*.   The first example with the *e* of *goode* silent is a good iambic line.

It is customary to say that the fifteenth and sixteenth-century editions of Chaucer were defective because the editors had failed to understand Chaucer's treatment of final *-e*.   From what has been said in this and the preceding chapters, I think it is the nineteenth-century scholars rather than the early editors who misunderstood Chaucer.   I have examined the printed texts of Chaucer by Caxton, W. de Worde, Pynson, Thynne (1542, 1561), Islip (1598), Speght (1687), and Urry (1721).   In general there perhaps tends to be a slight vulgarization of Chaucer's verse but the rhetorical pattern remains fundamentally the same as I have tried to show, and many of the readings are those which have been restored in the Manly-Rickert text.   The edition of Adam Islip (1598) contains dedicatory verses originally written

for Henry VIII. It is clear that their author understood the
rhythmical tradition, because the verses are not iambic decasyllables, but are obviously rhythmical. Not until we come to
the edition of Urry (1721) do we begin to depart from the rhythmical pattern. Urry proposed, as I have mentioned, to correct
the text of Chaucer. He "found it was the opinion of some learned
Men that Chaucer's Verses originally consisted of an equal
number of Feet; and he himself was perswaded that Chaucer
made them exact Metre, and therefore he proposed . . . to restore
him . . . *to his feet again.*" It is interesting, of course, that this
idea of exact feet is thought of when Pope's heroic couplets were
admired for their finish and when to be thought "correct" was
the highest praise. And it is in Urry that we first find *sweté*,
smalé, allé, strangé marked as dissyllabic. The subsequent route
is clear: to Tyrwhitt, Child, Schipper, Ten Brink, *et alia.*
And notice that it was the "learned men" and not the poets
that made the suggestion.

From the foregoing it is obvious that I no longer believe valid
the rules for the pronunciation of final -*e* in adjectives or nouns
that I proposed in my earlier "Chaucer's Final -E in Rhyme".
As I have mentioned, those rules were based on the assumption
that the iambic decasyllabic theory was valid, which, we have
seen, it was not.

It would be possible to multiply examples to support my thesis.
But I am not at this time concerned with all of Chaucer's subtleties. I think, however, that a careful study of his practice in
the several tales might reveal differences between his earliest
and his latest when his craftsmanship was at its most mature.
It is important now to examine the work of those poets who
looked upon Chaucer as their master to see if the rhetorical or
rhythmical theory of prosody can be applied to their work.
We know that the iambic theory fails miserably. It seems
strange that this fact alone would not have aroused doubt
among linguistic scholars. It is not with the Chinese alone,
however, that ancestor worship still plays an important role in
one's thinking.

CHAPTER FIVE

THE TESTIMONY OF THE MANUSCRIPTS:
CHAUCER'S FOLLOWERS

IN the first three chapters of the present study I attempted to clear away many of the misconceptions concerning the basis of Chaucer's prosody. In Chapter Four I endeavoured to show what the actual nature of Chaucer's prosody was. In the present chapter, I shall endeavour to show that the system of prosody used by Chaucer was understood and in a general way, at least, practised by his followers. Nowhere does the iambic theory more clearly reveal that it was a "Teutonic method of establishing out of thin air a hypothetical *typus*" than in the treatment of Chaucer's followers by the nineteenth-century scholars. Let us examine first the work of Hoccleve, the poet who, scholars believe, probably knew Chaucer and possibly worked under him. To say, as Furnivall said of him, that he did not understand Chaucer's prosody seems highly unrealistic indeed. It is not the disciples of Mr. Eliot or Mr. Pound or Mr. Williams who fail to understand their prosody; it is the professors. Several years ago, for example, I witnessed a most shocking display on the part of a professor of his inability to grasp the newer rhythms and to cover his ineptitude by means of ridicule. He was attacking the poetry of Mr. Auden, Mr. Spender, and Mr. Day Lewis, and was completely oblivious to their rhythms, evident from the manner in which he desecrated their verses in his reading. And it would have been as difficult for the majority of the late nineteenth-century professors to appreciate Chaucer's rhythms as it was for this twentieth-century professor to do justice to the work of many of our moderns. I do not intend to make any extravagant claims for Hoccleve's stature as a poet, but I do claim that his mastery of Chaucer's idiom was greater than has been acknowledged. Unfortunately there is no good edition of Hoccleve and I must perforce depend on the testimony of the MSS.

In his edition Furnivall castigated Hoccleve so violently that Hoccleve has dwelt under a shadow ever since. He denied him any degree of metrical competence whatever: "Hoccleve's metre is poor," he said. "So long as he can count ten syllables by his fingers, he is content. . . . He constantly thwarts the natural run of his line by putting stress on a word that shouldn't bear it, or using a strong syllable as a weak one. . . . He turns the pronoun *hire* her, into two syllables. . . . Hoccleve often breaks a measure awkwardly with his pause, as in 'Wiste I what / good freend / tell on what is best'. . . . He not only lets the metrical pause stop the cutting-off of a final -*e* before a vowel or *h*, but he also keeps *e* in other parts of the line: 'To helthë him profytë / ne god qweeme'." (I, xli. xlii). These are serious charges indeed to bring against so popular a poet as Hoccleve. But was Furnivall correct ? It has been suggested to me in all seriousness by a prominent linguist, who evidently supports Furnivall's opinion of Hoccleve, that the change in the treatment of final -*e* between Chaucer's death and Hoccleve's poems (about ten years) was so rapid that Chaucer's English was like that of a foreign language to Hoccleve. No person with any understanding of the rhythms of English or of the persistence of English dialects could entertain such a statement seriously. Even during periods of war language does not change rapidly. Is it not more than probable that the disappearance of final -*e* had already occurred ? But what facts can we bring forward in defence of Hoccleve ? I have been accused of setting up straw men to knock down. I admit that there are many straw men, but it is the linguists who have set them up for me. So long as they continue to neglect the aesthetic aspects of the materials with which they deal, they will continue to set up straw men.

The most positive test we can put forward for the pronunciation or non-pronunciation of final -*e*, apart from the testimony of historical grammar, is its treatment in a poem whose rhythms are definite and predetermined. We have such a poem in Carleton Brown's collection of medieval religious lyrics. The rhythm—a strong trochaic tetrameter—is obviously dictated by the Latin lyric "Stabat iuxta Christi crucem". Any deviations would immediately become suspect. No. 4 in Brown's *English Lyrics of the Thirteenth Century* begins in iambic tetrameter, but shifts to trochaic tetrameter in stanza 2. Stanza 1 begins as follows:

> at leveli leor wid spald ischent
> at feire fel wid s[cur]ges rend—

The *e* of *feire* was probably sounded. The situation is the same in No. 48. In *riche levedies, proude ʒong, harde stoundes, foule ping*, w*ikke roun*, the *e may* or *may not* have been sounded; and in No. 65 in *rode tree* it probably was. I agree with Weymouth that final *e* during this earlier period *may* be sounded if the rhythm so requires. Turning to the selection from the lyrics of the fourteenth century, we find it readily apparent that during the early part of the century the *e* could still be sounded, particularly in the South. Not until we come to the later selections do we begin to find scribal evidence of the disappearance of the pronunciation of *e* in adjectives in weak position. In No. 93— "An Orison to the Trinity"—many *e*'s are omitted from the text that should be there if it were still sounded. It is even possible here, too, that the *e* could or could not be sounded according to the demands of the metre. In No. 132—"Quia Amore Langueo" —however, the stanzaic pattern would indicate that by the close of the century the *e* had ceased being pronounced:

> I longe for love of man my brother,
> I am hys vokete to voyde his vyce;
> I am hys moder—I can none other—
> Why shuld I my dere chylde dispyce ?
> Yif he me wrathe in diverse wyse,
> Though flesshes freelte fall me fro
>
> Yet must we rewe hym tyll he ryse,
>   Quia amore langueo.

In this same poem we also have:

> I byd, I byde in grete longyng,
> I love, I loke when man woll crave.

The *e* of the adjectives in *dere chylde*, *diverse wyse*, and *grete longyng* could not be sounded. If the reader thinks that these are insufficient examples, I can only suggest that there are few poems in Brown's collection in the London dialect, most of them being from the conservative South and South-west.

In his selection from the fifteenth century the evidence is complete that *e* of adjectives in a weak position had ceased to be sounded. No. 32—"An Orison to Our Lady by the Seven Joys", in *rime royal*, affords several examples:

> Schew ye youre myght, your grace & your goodnesse
> To youre sarvant that lythe in grete dystresse.

6, 7

Hertes sorow and verray unyarde dred
Maketh me fle to youre grace for socowre
ffor ye never yit faylid none at nede—
youre grete mercy so fre is every owre.
Now swete lady, ryght as ʒe be the flowre
Of all womene . . .

15—20

So, too, does No. 28—"Regina Celi Letare, II":

O kynde curatrix, to thi caytif kyd,
To cure oure sore þou keptyst a corn.
Within thy bowelys thow bare a bryd,
The blessydest blossum þat ever was born,
Oure holy lorde on the was hydde.
By hyrying of a Angels horn,
A mansuete message was the amydde,
Godys mother to be called at euyn & morn.

13—20

Although both of the foregoing poems are in decasyllables, it is quite obvious that they are not iambic decasyllables.

Now the important thing about these illustrations from the thirteenth to the fifteenth centuries is that they reveal that the poet easily makes the adjustment in the matter of sounding or not sounding the final *e* without disturbing the rhythms. I cannot but believe that so irresponsible a statement as that Chaucer's language would be like that of a foreign language to his disciple was the result of passionate statement in a heated discussion when logic was lost sight of.   One other statement was made which I was surprised to find still being repeated: that Chaucer's treatment of final *e* was exactly like that of Goethe.   But of that I have said enough.

I regret that I must so often indulge in seeming digressions from the main line of argument.   But I have felt it necessary to answer many of the irrelevancies that have been posed by the many scholars who find it difficult to believe that so much of Chaucer scholarship may have been built on unsupported hypotheses.   Unsupported hypotheses are not, however, unique in the humanities.   Engineers, natural scientists and biological scientists constantly are confronted with them.

But to return to Hoccleve.   Hoccleve was a popular poet, as the number of MSS attests.   In HM 744. f. 25 ff. is his *Invocio ad Patrem*, in which the virgule is used.   Many of the lines could be read as iambic decasyllables; they can also be read observing the rhetorical stresses.   The following line cannot be read metrically, but it reads well rhythmically:

O sweet love / Withinne a litel space   —6: 5

The following, if read rhythmically has a beauty of movement; if read iambically it is monotonous:

(rhythmically)

(metrically)

And dyde / for our trespas and offence

—II: 7

In the first instance it contains nine syllables; in the second eleven.   It is impossible to think of the length of the unstressed final *e* in *offence* as similar to French mute *e*.

Let us look at the entire stanza.   It, too, has a beauty of movement when read rhythmically, a movement which is a little more elegiac than that we associate with Chaucer's *rime royal*.

He that is meek / and spotless Innocent

That for our gift / to dye / nothyng dradd

Which to his deeth / Was maad obedient

And in his torment / ful greet delyt hadd

Remembrynge / how the synful foltes badd

Redempt sholde be / thurgh his passion

Out of the daunger of the feend adoun[9]

—13

The *Lepistre de Cupid* (f. 39 v. ff.), which Furnivall found wholly impossible and in which Skeat "touched up the final *e*'s," reads well rhythmically:

And passyng alle londes / on this yle

That clept is Albion they moost compleyne

They seyn that there is croppe (?) and root of gyle

So can the men dissimulen and feyne

With standyng dropes in her yen tweyne

Whan that hir herte / feelith no distresse

To blynde women with her doublenesse

—3

As poetry, of course, it is pretty feeble.

The various MSS of the *Regement of Princes* throw better light on Hoccleve's versification than do the foregoing illustrations. In HM 135 [Phillips MS 8980] we have an interesting phenomenon. No mark is used in stanza one, the · is used in stanza two; both the · and virgule appear in stanza three, and from that point on only the virgule. If we ignore the virgule many lines could be read as iambic decasyllables, but they read better when read to make the accents correspond to the rhetorical sense. Since we have seen that there is no basis for the iambic decasyllabic theory, Hoccleve could scarcely employ what did not exist. Must we assume that in a beautifully written MS either

the scribe or the poet was incompetent, or as I have repeatedly
asked, should we question the basis of the prosody ? The following is from HM 135. The reader should notice carefully how my
scansion is supported by the evidence of other MSS of the same
passage.

This ylke nyght / y walwod to and fro

Sekyng reste / but certeynly sche

Apperyd not / for thoght my cruel fo

hadde chased her and slepe   a wey fro me

and for I scholde / not alone be

Agayne my lust / Wache profryd his service

and I admytted hym / in hevy wyse

—II

In Sloane 1212, this stanza is as follows:

> This ilk nyght I walwed too and froo
> sechyng reste = but certeynly she
> apperid noght = for þogh my cruel foo
> had chased hire = and slep away fro me
> and for I shuld not allone bee
> Ageyn my lust Wacche profred his servyse
> and I admytted hym in hevy wise

In comparing Harleian 4826, Bodleian Digby 185, Bodleian
Douce 158, Bodleian Rawlinson Poet 10, Cambridge, St. John's
College, 223, Sloane 1212, and Trinity College 602 (R. 3. 22),
we find many variations in spelling: *in* and *inne*, *ilk* and *ilke*,
had and *hadde*, *right* and *riȝte*, *rest* and *reste*, and so forth. Instead of *solitarie*, *adversarie* and *tributarie* (st. 13) Bodleian

Digby 185 has solitayre, adversayre, and tributayre.   In spite
of textual differences, however, every text reads well rhythmically
and the stresses fall on the identical vowels, although every text
is often crude metrically.   Bodleian Douce 158, for example,
illustrates the scribe's use of the virgule:

At Chestres Inne / right fast by the stronde	5
This der I seyn / may no wyght make his boost	12
My tremblyng hert / so grete gastnesse hadde	20
Sechyng rest / but certeynly she	72

In an actual test count of the position of the virgule in 100 lines
of Hoccleve, we find that his distribution is similar to that of
Chaucer.   In lines 8—107 ("Thomas Hoccleve[s Complaint]",
Furnivall, I, 95—99), we have after the second syllable, 1;
after the third, 10; after the fourth, 38; the fifth, 21; the sixth,
12; the seventh, 3; the eighth, 2; with no virgule, 13.   This
is what we should expect from a disciple.   He has caught the
obvious surface music, but he had not been able to invest the
music with the vitality of the master.   He neither has Chaucer's
fine ear for subtle variation in stresses, nor does he have the
same feeling for words in juxtaposition that is one of Chaucer's
great qualities.   In other words Hoccleve had caught the surface
rhythms of Chaucer's verse but did not have within himself the
ability to feel them deeply, and incidentally, to modify them to
fit his own inner needs.   The farther from Chaucer that we move,
the greater will be the vulgarization of his prosody.   This will
be clear when we examine Lydgate's use of the virgule.

  Lydgate was not much of a poet, it is true, but it is a great
injustice to him to think that he could not write correct verse.
The trouble I find with him is not that so many of his verses
have broken backs (because I do not think they do), but that he
possesses so little subtlety.   Read rhythmically his verses are
smooth, too smooth.   They go along at a jog-trot pace that is
fatiguing.   It would be the type of verses, however, that would
please those making some pretence at culture.   They would,
like the general reader of poetry today, resent lines that were
irregular, but they would not demand too great subtlety.   The
MSS of Lydgate's *Fall of Princes* are numerous, and for the most
part, beautifully written and illuminated.   Oxf. Bodle. e Museo
1, B.M. Additional 21410, Oxf. Bodl. Hatton 2 do not employ

the virgule, but Oxf. Bodl. Rawlinson C. 448 does, once the scribe
is well under way.   The first stanza, excruciatingly dull when
read rhythmically, is impossible metrically:

> He that some tyme dyd his delygence
> The boke of Bochas in frensh to translate
> Out of latyne he called is Laurence
> That tyme remembred treuly and þe date
> There whan kyng John þorough his mortal fate
> Was presoner brought un to the region
> Whan he be gan this translacion

As we move farther into the work, however, the double virgule
makes its appearance.   If we observe it in our reading, we realize
the sing-song quality of the verse.   Notice that with Lydgate
the position of the virgule is more regular than with Hoccleve
and falls predominantly after the fourth syllable:

> ♪ | ♩♪ | ♩♩ | ♩· ♩· | ♩ ♩♪ | ♩
> And in Achaia // it ded most damage

> | ♩ ♪ | ♩· ♩· | ♪ | ♩ ♪ | ♩ ♪ | ♩
> Tyme of Jacob // the patriark notable

> ♪ | ♪· | ♩· ♩· | ♩ ♪ | ♩· ♩· | ♩
> And this deluge // with his wawes rage

> | ♩· | ♩· ♩· | ♩· ♩· | ♪ | ♩ ♩ | ♩· ♩· | ♩
> Slough lordis manye // & pryncis honur able

> ♪ | ♩· | ♩· ♩· | ♩♪ | ♩♩♪ | ♩
> ffor dame ffortune // is so deceyv able

> ♪ | ♩· ♩· | ♩· | ♩ ♪ | ♩ ♪ | ♩
> That she sumwhile // whom she list dis deyne

> ♪ | ♩ ♩♪ | ♩· | ♩ ♩♪ | ♩ ♪ | ♩
> Can folk assaile // with a flood sod eyne

This same regularity is observable in his "Danse Macabre"
(Lansdowne 699, fol. 41b):

> | ♩· | ♩· ♩· | ♩ ♩♪ | ♩· ♩· | ♩
> O creatures / that ben resonable

> ♪ | ♩ ♩♪ | ♩· ♩· | ♩ ♪ | ♩♩♪ | ♩
> the lyf desiryng / which is eternall

> ♪ | ♩· ♩· | ♩· | ♩ ♪ | ♩ ♪ | ♩
> ye may seen heer / doct[r]ine ful not able

♪ | ♪· ♪· | ♩· | ♩   ♪ | ♩ ♪ | ♩
your liff to lede / which that is mortall

| ♪· | ♪· ♪· | ♩· | ♩♪ | ♪· ♪· | ♩
therby to lerne / in especi all

♪ | ♪· ♪· | ♩   ♪ | ♩   ♪ | ♩ ♪ | ♩
how ye shal trace / the dance which that ye see

♪ | ♩   ♪ | ♪· ♪· | ♩ ♪ | ♩ ♪ | ♩
for deth ne sparith / hih nor lowe degree

Mr. C. S. Lewis arrived independently at the pattern of Lydgate's verse indicated in the foregoing. Mr. Henry Bergen, the editor of the *Fall of Princes*, believed that the broken-backed lines were caused by Lydgate's failure to understand Chaucer's treatment of final *e*. The simpler explanation is that he failed to understand Chaucer's flexibility in the use of the virgule. We do not know, of course, whether Chaucer used the virgule in his holographs, but the fact that the best MSS do employ it gives some support to the idea already proposed that the scribes were following his markings. The fact that it appears only in Wyatt's MSS in his own hand lends support to the idea that it was the poet's and not the scribe's mark.

In the first 100 lines of Lydgate's *Siege of Thebes* (Erdmann, 2 vols., London, 1911 I, 1—6), the distribution of the virgule reveals that Lydgate has no flexibility. We find no use of it, for example, after the first, second, seventh, or eighth syllables, as we do in Chaucer and Hoccleve. We have after the third, 15; after the fourth, 73; after the fifth, 8; after the sixth, 2; one line with no virgule, and one line with two (after syllables 1 and 4). Or 96 of the virgules fall about midway in the line. No wonder the verse is monotonous.

The thing that happened to Chaucer's beautiful flexibility in the hands of Lydgate, writing for a less sophisticated audience than that of Chaucer, is the same that happened to Pope's heroic couplets in the hands of pedestrian versifiers and to the beautiful rhythms of Tennyson's "Ulysses", say, in the hands of a Longfellow. These more obvious rhythms, however, would be more popular with the rich patrons than would the subtler music of a master. We have only to study the prosody of some of our contemporary verse that has achieved the "best-seller" popularity to see that the rhythms are not so subtle as those of Eliot, Ransom, Stevens, Pound, and others.

But let us continue with examples from the fifteenth and sixteenth centuries to see how the rhythmical theory fits the facts. And it is facts we are interested in and not the "Teutonic method of establishing out of thin air a hypothetical *typus*." "The Libelle of Englysche Polycye" (Ed. by Geo. Warner, Oxford, 1926) provides evidence from 1436. Unfortunately the virgule is not used, but a musical notation will indicate competent verse with greater variety than that of Lydgate. I have indicated where I think the virgule might fall in the following:

♪ |♪. ♪. | ♩ | ♩ ♪|♪. ♪. | ♩
Shall any prynce / what so be hys name

| ♩ ♪ | ♪. ♪. | ♩. | ♩ ♪|♩ (♪)
Whiche hath nobles / moche lyche to oures

♪ | ♩ ♪ | ♩ ♪ | ♪. ♪. | ♪. ♪. | ♩
Be lorde of see / and Flemmynges to our blame

| ♪. | ♪. | ♪. ♪. ♪ |♪. ♪. | ♩ ♪ | ♩(♪)
Stoppe us / take us / and so make fade the floures

♪ |♪. ♪. | ♩ | ♩ ♪ | ♩. | ♩ ♪ | ♩ (♪)
Of Englische state / and disteyne oure honoures

♪ | ♪. ♪. | ♩ ♪|♩ ♪ | ♩ ♪ | ♩
For cowardyce allas / hit shulde so be

| ♪. ♪. ♪|♪. ♪. |♪. ♪. | ♪. ♪. |♩
Therfore / I gynne to write now / of the see

—43—49

Although there are an increasing number of iambs (♪| ♩) in the verses, any attempt to read them, even with the usual allowable substitutions, falls down. A later passage from the same work is less regular and can only be read rhythmically. It is less smooth than the foregoing:

| ♪. | ♩ ♪| ♩ ♪|♩ ♪|♩♩|♩
Kepe than the see abought / in speciall

| ♩ ♪ |♪. ♪. | ♩ ♪ | ♩. | ♩
Whiche / of England / is the rounde well

|♪. ♪. |♪. ♪.| ♪. |♪. ♪. | ♪ ♪ |♪. ♪.
As though England were lykened / to a cit e

♪ ♪ | ♩ ♪ | ♪· ♪· | ♩ ♪ | ♩

And the wall environ / were the see

| ♪· | ♩·   ♪ | ♩ | ♪ ♪ ♪ | ♩ ♪ | ♪· ♪·

Kepe than the see / that is the wall of Englond

♪ | ♪· ♪· | ♪· ♪· | ♩   ♪ | ♪ ♩ | ♩

And than is Englond kepte / by goddes sonde

♪ | ♪· ♪· | ♪ ♩ | ♩ | ♪ | ♩ ♪ | ♩

That as for ony thinge / that is wythoute

| ♪· ♪· | ♪· | ♩ ♪ | ♩   ♪ | ♩ ♪ | ♩

England were than at ease / wythouten doute

♪ | ♩·   ♪· | ♩ ♪ | ♩ | ♪ ♪ ♪ | ♪· ♪·

And thus shuld everi lande / one with another

| ♩ ♪ | ♪ ♪ ♪ | ♪· ♪· | ♩   ♪ | ♪· ♪·

Entrecomen as brother / wyth his brother

—1092—1101

In *The Kingis Quair* (Ed. by Lawson, London, 1910, W. Mackay Mackenzie, 1939), we have the occasional use of the virgule. The exact date of the work is unknown, but it probably lies between 1440—1480. Here is stanza 59:

| ♪· | ♪· ♪· | ♪· ♪· | ♪ ♩ | ♩ ♪ | ♩·

Gyf thou suld sing wele euer in thy lyve

| ♪ ♪ ♪ | ♩ ♪ | ♩ ♪ | ♩ ♪ | ♩

Here is in fay the tyme and eke the space

| ♪· | ♪· ♪· | ♪· ♪· | ♩ ♪ | ♩ ♪ | ♩

Quhat wastow than sum bird may cum and stryve

♪ | ♪· ♪· | ♩ ♪ | ♩ ♪ | ♩ ♪ | ♩

In song with the / the maistry to purchase

| ♪· | ♩ ♪ | ♩ ♪ | ♪· | ♪· | ♪ ♪ | ♩

Suld thou than cesse / It were grete schame al lace

♪ | ♩ ♪ | ♪· | ♪· | ♪ ♪ ♪ | ♪· | ♪· ♪·

And here to wyn gree happily for euer

| ♪ ♪ ♪ | ♩ ♪ | ♩   ♪ | ♪· ♩· | ♪· ♩·

Here is the tyme to syng / or ellis neuer

The stanza has a beautiful rhythmical movement but can be read as strongly iambic. One of the characteristics of Chaucer's verse, as I have pointed out, is the frequent use of two strong stresses in juxtaposition. I find a similar practice by this poet. I read the first two syllables in the first, second, third, and fifth lines; and the fourth and fifth syllables in the first line; and the seventh and eighth syllables of the sixth line as stressed, or as spondees. The last three syllables of the seventh line form an amphibrach ($\smile$ / $\smile$). The poet has caught the true Chaucerian ring. Actually, of course, we should not even speak of feet. To test this similarity, let the reader turn to *Troilus and Criseyde*, V, 1835—1848 and read them without sounding the *e*'s, and he will have an almost identical music. The first line should be read as follows:

♪ | ♩· | ♩· | ♩♪ ♩|♩ ♪|♩
O yonge fresshe folkes he or she

Let us pass quickly over some of the better known poems of the early sixteenth century. The following from Alexander Barclay's *The Ship of Fools* (1509) has a Chaucerian movement. Lines three, four, and six call for a rhythmical reading:

Why sholde I stody to hurt my wyt therby
Or trouble my mynde with stody excessive
Sythe many as whiche stody right besely
And yet thereby shall they never thryve
The fruyt of wysdom can they not contryve
And many to stody so moche are inclynde
That utterly they fall out of theyr mynde.

(Ed. by Patterson, 1874, p. 21)

Nott (*Poems of Wyatt and Surrey*, 1815) quotes a stanza of Barclay from a MS which employed the double virgule:

I have advanced // to glorious laud and fame
Paul that was Consul // of the empire Romaine
Which divers nations wan // increasing his name
To the said Romains // triumph and laud sovereign
And tho' they suffered // peril and great pain
Yet hath the love and meed // of me virtue
Not suffered them // hard changes to eschew

—clxxviii

Stephen Hawes, "The convercyn of swerers" (1530) demands a rhythmical reading, and given such, it is competent verse:

By theyr weytynge doth to us appere

The famous actes of many a champyon

In the courte of fame renowned fayre and clere

And some endyted theyr entencyon

Cloked in colours harde in construccyon

Specyally poets under cloudy fygures

Covered the trouthe of all theyr scryptures

Nott also illustrates the use of the virgule or a similar mark in Hawes:

O master Lydgate . the most dulcet spring
Of famous Rhetoric . with ballad royal
The chief original . of my learning
What vaileth it . on you for to call
Me for to aid . now in especial
Sithen your body . is now wrapt in chest
I pray God to give . your soul good rest

—clxxvi, clxxvii

The MS which I have examined of Thomas Feyld's "A contraversye bytwene a lover and a jaye" (1522) employs no virgule. It would be a simple matter, however, to insert one to assist in the rhythmical reading; metrically it is quite obviously impossible:

Who lyketh thy sentence / and pondereth it ryght
Correctynge well / in his remembraunce
Know may he / truely / that by a lady bryght
Thou was compyled / by pastymes pleasaunce
Such great unkyndnesse / which caused varyance
Was shewed to a lover / called F. C.
Her name also / begynneth with A. B.

In John Heywood's "The pardoner and the frere" (1533) the virgule is used regularly:

Mary that shall we tyre / even strayt way
I defy the churle preest / & there be no mo than thou
I wyll not go with the / I make god a vow
We shall se fyrst which is the stronger
God hath sent be bonys I do thee not fere

I could cite further examples from Edward Gosynhall's "The prayse of all women" and "The lyfe of seynt Gregoryes mother", from Osborn Bokenam (c. 1450), Thomas Norton (c. 1477), and others, but the story would be the same.   Except, as we have seen in the example from "The Kingis Quhair", there has been a steady vulgarization in the rhythms, although the overall pattern has remained clear.   Their rhythms reflect no deep convictions on the part of the poets, nor do they spring to life because of the subject matter.   They are superficial and pedestrian, rather than integral.

Let us turn now to the poetry of Thomas Wyatt to see if he is at the end of a tradition, at the beginning of a new one, or possibly both.   I am indebted to Miss A. K. Foxwell's edition of his poems from MSS in his own hand and to Mr. Richard Harrier's edition (unpublished) from the same sources for such an opportunity.   It is common knowledge that Wyatt's poems printed in Tottel's *Miscellany* had been edited to conform to a metrical theory of prosody—a theory possibly inspired by the great revival in humanistic studies under way at the sister universities of Cambridge and Oxford.   I have accepted Miss Foxwell's dating of the poems which I have used.   In "Love's Arraignment", one of Wyatt's earliest poems (1527), it is clear that he worked within the English tradition which we have been illustrating.   But I do not think any of the particular illustrations was his model.   It is impossible to scan "Love's Arraignment"

("Myne olde dere En'my") metrically without receiving the impression that it is halting incompetent verse; read rhythmically it has beauty:

O ! small hony much aloes & gall

In bitternes have my blynde lyfe taisted

His fals swetenes that torneth as a ball

With the amourous dawnce have made me traced

And where I had my thought, & mynde ataced,

from all erthely frailnes, & vain pleasure,

he toke me from rest and set me in error

I, 67 [Harrier, 346]

Rondeau 7, a translation from Petrarch, also from 1527, indicates that for his rhythms Wyatt returned to the master Chaucer and not to any vulgar imitation. Probably readily available to him was one of Pynson's editions of Chaucer—1492, 1498, or more likely, that of 1526. Except for the omission of a few unaccented prepositions or articles the rhythmical scansion of this is identical with that of the Hengwrt or Ellesmere. For his later work Thynne's edition (1532) employing the virgule was available. The Pynson and Thynne—at least so much of them as I have examined—are almost identical from the point of view of text. Here is the opening of Rondeau 7:

Goo burnyng sighes / unto the frosen hert

goo, breke the ise whiche pites paynfull dert

myght never perse, and if mortall prayer

in hevyn may be herd at last I desire

that deth or mercy be ende of my smert

Reduced to metrical notation, what do we find ? Wyatt uses spondees as frequently as Chaucer. In the foregoing two stresses appear in juxtaposition in the first foot of the first, second, and third verses, and in the fourth of the fifth. Trochees are more common, too, and occur in the third and fourth feet of the third verse, and the second, third, and fourth foot of the fourth verse. We must always remember, however, that in neither Italian, French, nor English poetry was the term foot really applicable. Convenient though it be from long use, it is inaccurate, and modern prosodists are abandoning the term.

If Rondeau 4 ("Helpe me to seke") antedates Pynson's edition of 1526, there is every indication that Wyatt had not studied the earlier editions. This rondeau shows Wyatt strug- gling with his rhythms. It was not until he had studied Chaucer's verse carefully that he seems to have mastered the subtleties of the rhythmical prosody. Wyatt's use of the virgule lends additional support to the theory that it was a rhetorical and not a metrical mark. The only poems in the MSS that employ the virgule are, as I have said, those in Wyatt's own hand. This raises the question whether the presence of the virgule in the Hengwrt and Ellesmere arose from the scribes' use of Chaucer's holograph for their copy. One would like to think so, but we must not erect a system on the practice of one poet as the nineteenth-century linguistic scholars were more than willing to do. Of one thing we may be certain. Wyatt did not think of the single verse as the unit. The virgule does not appear in every verse, nor often in a great percentage of the verses. It does appear where it can be of aid to the reader. The following

illustrations speak for themselves to those who can hear and are
from Poems 171 ("Love to gyve law"), 172 "(O Lord sins in my
mowght thy myghty name"), 176 ("O Lord as I the have both
prayd and pray"), and 178 "(Rew on me lord for thy goodnes"),
all from the text of Richard Harrier:

> afore his brest / frawted w^t disease
> off stormy syghes / his chere coloured lyk clay
> dressyd upryght / sekyng to conterpese
> $\qquad$ —171; 68—70, p. 386

> O Lord I dred / and y^t I did not dred
> I me repent / and euermore desyre
> the the to dred / I open here and spred
> my faute to the / but y^u for thi goodnes
> $\qquad$ —172: 11—14, p. 387

> Oh dyuerse er the chastysinges off syn
> in mete / in drink / in breth y^t man doth blow
> In slepe / in wach / in fretyng still w^t in
> $\qquad$ —174: 65—67, p. 398

> nor me correct in wrathfull castigation
> ffor that thi arrows off fere / off terrour
> of sword / of sekenes / off famine & fyre
> stikkes diepe in me / I lo from myn errour
> Ame plongid up / as horse owt of the myre
> w^t strok off spurr / such is thi hand on me
> y^t in my fleshe for terrour of thy yre
> $\qquad$ —176: 6—12, p. 402

In individual lines it marks the "cadence": "This song is
endid / david did stint his voyce" (175: 1, p. 400), "Carffd in
the rokk / w^t Iyes and handes on hygh (175: 15, p. 400), "first
dasd his Iyes / and forder forth he stertes (171: 5, p. 382).
For Sonnet 2 ("The longe love"), Sonnet 4 ("Was I never yet
of your love greved"), Epigram 1 ("Who hath herd") the model
is obvoiusly Chaucer.   Satire 1 ("My Owne John Poynz") is one
more example to show the traditional influence. There is a definite
pause in the middle of the line.   When we come to Epigram 20
[Harrier, Poem 109] ("Tagus, fare well)" (c. 1540, 1) it is evident
that a new influence is at work.   Here we have a regular iambic line:

> Tagus, fare well, y^t westward w^t thy strems
> torns up the grayns off gold alredy tyrd

w^t spurr and sayle for I go seke the tems
gaynward the sonne y^t shewth her welthi pryd
and to the town wych brutus sowght by drems
like bendyd mone doth lend her lusty syd.
My king my Contry alone for whome I lyve
Of myghty love the wings for this me gyve
—Harrier, p. 282

Wyatt has accepted the new tradition introduced by Surrey, who in Italy had fallen under the spell of the humanists who were so fired with desire to emulate the ancients. In this desire the older medieval tradition was lost sight of although English poets like Stephen Hawes, John Heywood, Gascoigne, Spenser, and others continued to have an essentially correct understanding of what Chaucer did. We might almost say that the "learned" poetry became metrical, the popular remained rhythmical.

This is one explanation. Miss Ing (*E.L.*, n. 138) has suggested another, pertaining particularly to Wyatt. It is her belief that it was Wyatt's "love and practice of song which cause his difficulties with sonnet form . . . and it may well be that he tended to think of sonnet lines as though they were song lines." Whether he carried the hemistich lines in his mind, or whether it was his love of song makes little real difference—both are rhythmical rather than metrical. It was not until "learned men" of the eighteenth century tried to fit Chaucer into the classical tradition that we began to lose sight of the tradition in which he did work. To review briefly: Urry began it in 1721, Tyrwhitt contributed to it in 1775, but merely threw out the suggestion that perhaps Chaucer used the *endecasillabo*. Nothing came of these suggestions, possibly because of the very able refutation of the suggestion by Nott in 1815. It was not until Child's "Observations" (1863) that the scholars upholding the metrical theory began to obtain a following. Always, however, there have been the few who have been more concerned with facts rather than with unsupported theories posited on nebulous foundations. The great work of Manly-Rickert on the *Canterbury Tales* cannot be overestimated. In spite of the desire of many scholars for that text, no inexpensive student's edition is available, nor is likely to be soon. When we do have it, however, I hope that the virgule will be inserted or indicated, because it is a rhetorical mark, and as such, is a great aid to a person to whom the rhythmical theory is unfamiliar. Readers familiar with our best modern poetry, however, need have no trouble, because as has often been pointed out by others, the work of the best modern poets is often rhythmical. Whereas in our earlier poetry it was the popular poet who remained rhythmical, today he remains metrical. But the forces at work among poets today are the same that have always existed: there is the beginning of a tradition, its perfection, and its decline. Chaucer brought the rhythmical tradition to its greatest pitch of perfection.

It is not difficult to understand, however, why many linguistic scholars will view the rhythmical theory with suspicion. Their measuring-stick becomes less rigid than easy thinking might prefer it to be, and it is of use only to those with a highly developed aesthetic sense.

In the pursuit of facts for the present study of the rhythmical tradition I have sought from the sceptics some account of those things I would have to prove to convince them. Although I have answered every one, I have no doubt that rather than go through the effort to understand the rhythmical theory they will invent new hurdles. The burden of proof is now on the sceptics to show where the foregoing arguments are weak. I have not been concerned with anything but the prosody. But I am also grateful to the sceptics. Without them I should probably have remained satisfied with my earlier treatment of final *e* in rhyme, unrealistic though I now realize that to have been. As it is, I have learned more about the prosody of the Middle Ages than at first I had any inkling of. It has been a pleasure to realize that Chaucer possessed a subtlety of nuance that the iambic theory completely conceals and to confirm for myself on the basis of facts alone the theory of Chaucer's prosody that was the generally accepted theory until the era of Child, and Ten Brink. The great error of Child and many of the German investigators was that they forgot that language is a living thing and that a study of *schriftsprache* without reference to the spoken language can lead only to confusion. Conservative scholars like Weymouth insisted from the outset on the spoken English of Chaucer and not on the symbols on paper.

The present work was completed when I chanced upon Mr. John Speirs, *Chaucer the Maker*, a work with which I am in hearty accord. I agree with him that it is only as we concentrate on the aesthetic aspects of Chaucer, which American teachers of Chaucer generally do not do, that we begin to have an adequate sense of his subtlety and nuance. My original dissatisfaction arose from aesthetic reasons. Why was the final *e* pronounced at the end of the line when it was not pronounced under the same conditions within ? The next step was to question the aesthetic justification of retaining so many *e*'s for metrical reasons. Once those were disposed of, Chaucer's place in the tradition of English poetry and his relations with his contemporaries became clear. Although he tended to regularize the length of the line and to avoid insistent alliteration, the movement is that of *Piers Plowman, Sir Gawayn*, Gower, and others—it is the movement of a highly developed English speech.

REFERENCES

1. See, for example, P. Gurrey, *The Appreciation of Poetry* (London, 1935, p. 93) and passages dealing with the treatment of rhyme; and C. Day Lewis, *Poetry For You* (New York, 1947, Chapter IV).

2. The italics are mine. Many modern linguists have so accustomed their ears to this all but intolerable monotony that they find Chaucer unpleasant without it. It was this monotony plus the fact that the final *-e* in rhyme destroyed the essential prose rhythm—particularly noticeable in the *Troilus*—that first led me to begin my investigations. In other words, it was an aesthetic dissatisfaction with the currently accepted pronunciation that prompted me to seek authority for a reading that was more congenial.

3. Furnivall could not have known, of course, of the methods of the scribes in the lay workshops.

4. Payne was one of the outstanding scholars in England of Anglo-Norman French. It was his contention that Lowell did not even know what was Anglo-Norman and what was not.

5. The reader should bear in mind that the notes refer to the work of a man who *died* in 1253. The notes are as follows:

l. 32.   "H gives this couplet thus:
            He moves ay ne be adrede
            Ne his ledone shall not be hed.

l. 331.   [þat þe wrecche prisoun]

"We should have here a line of only five syllables, were we not warranted by the A.S. *wrǽcca* to sound the final syllable of wrecche."

l. 830 [þat is, pruide, þa biginnynge
         And þe roote of al vuel þinge]

"As *biginnynge* is either the *nom.* or *acc.* in l. 829, it is clearly impossible that the final *e* should be sounded; and therefore the final *e* of þinge must not be pronounced.

"*Drihte, sb.*, lord, 27. The A.S. nominative was sometimes monosyllabic, but sometimes *drihten* or *dryhten* was used, as in Tat. we find *trohtin* and *truhtin*, and in Isid. Hisp. *druhtin*. It follows that the final *e* of *drihte*, as perhaps representing the termination *-en*, *may* be sounded, if the metre requires it.

Boþe, num. adj., both, 497. A line of five syllables in this metre would scarcely be tolerable; but the A.S. *begen*, O. Sax., *bede*, Du. and Ger. *beide*, etc., fully warrant us in taking the word as a dissyllable.

Wiþoute, wiþouten, prep., without, 4, 11, etc. The existence of the latter of these forms, like the A.S. *wiþutan*, shows that the final *e* of *wiþoute* may be sounded if the metre requires it."

We must remember, as I have suggested, that this work belonged to the late thirteenth century, and that we must *know* what the metre is.

6. In *Secular Lyrics of the XIV and XV Centuries* (Robbins, 1952) we have *blys* rhyming with *ys* (20: 6); *blysse* rhyming with *coronaberis* (52 : 6); *bliss* (133 : 19); *blys* rhyming with *nys* (150 : 4). This corroborates Payne's statement of the phonetic identity of *-s* and *-sse*.

7. I am indebted to Miss Mabel Dean, one of Manly's editorial assistants, for this statement.

8. A poet working in the rhythmical rather than a metrical tradition often displays a subtlety of ear that is beyond the reach of the ordinary reader. Fourteen consecutive drafts exist, for example, of William Carlos Williams's "The Sleeping Brute." One version might differ from its preceding solely by the manner in which the poet has broken up his statement into verses. It takes an exceedingly subtle ear to detect the difference in rhythmical value effected by the change.

9. As I have previously mentioned, every sensitive reader, aware that his stresses are rhetorical, will occasionally alter these stresses. In this stanza, for example, I originally read the opening lines as follows:

He that is meek / and spotless innocent

That for our gilt / to dye / nothyng dradd

Which to his death / Was maad obedient

And in his torment / ful greet delyt hadd

But I had not yet freed myself from what Pound called the manacles "of the goddam iamb".